"It really does take a village and if you don't already have one, this is a great place to start. A truly honest and inspiring behind the scenes look at pregnancy and motherhood. Any mama can relate to one, or all, of these beautifully candid experiences."
~ Cheryl Horne of Cheryl Anne Media | Business Developer | mama of two | https://cherylannemedia.com

"I am not a mom, nor is it something in my 'plan' and this book still spoke to me. The strength and awareness in this book is clear. You will truly know that 'You've Got This' after reading this book."
~ Ky-Lee Hanson, 4x best selling Amazon author | Owner of Golden Brick Road Publishing House | Serial Entrepreneur

"A beautiful, powerful and collective reminder to trust in our journey, and that our past does not have to paint our future."
~ Victoria Turner, Public Figure | Igniter of #PowerTribes | mama of three | http://www.yourpoweroutlet.com

"You Got This, Mama is uplifting and raw. The emotional truth of motherhood is fully exposed leaving you filled with overwhelming love and support. It's a must-read for every mother and mother to be!"
~ Tia Slightham of Tia Slightham Parenting Solutions | parenting coach | family consultant | mama of two | http://www.tiaslightham.com

"Raw truth that will touch a mom's heart and give rays of hope and connection. Real and inspirational."
~ Elaine Kaley, BSW, RSW Counsellor | Founder of Hungry for Hope Professional Counselling | mama of two | grandma of five

"Powerful, raw, empowering. A surefire way to know that you are NEVER alone in motherhood. This is a must read - the perspective, courage, wisdom, and strength provided to me by this book aided in my own healing as a first-time mum after a very traumatic first year."
~ Tania Moraes-Vaz, Editor | Coach | Coauthor "Dear Stress, I'm Breaking Up With You" & "On Her Plate" | mama of one

"The vulnerability, courage and strength of the women who share their stories in You've Got This, Mama is moving to the core. This book had me feel connected to each and every one of the mothers, it filled my heart up and made me proud to be a mother."
~ Christie Groom, Entrepreneur | Executive Regional Vice President, Arbonne International | mama of one

"A loving push to encourage you through one of the most beautiful endeavours, the emotion and strength is heartfelt and truly inspiring."
~ Victoria Chan Shearman of RED9INE | Entrepreneur | artist | mama of two

YOU'VE GOT THIS,
Mama

A MOTHER'S GUIDE TO EMBRACING THE CHAOS
& LIVING AN EMPOWERED LIFE

YOU'VE GOT THIS,
Mama

A MOTHER'S GUIDE TO EMBRACING THE CHAOS
& LIVING AN EMPOWERED LIFE

SABRINA GREER *featuring The Mama Tribe*

SARAH SECOR-MACELROY · JODIE TILLEY · ANGELA MUSCAT · CARRIE MAZZEI
KRISTIN HALLETT · HABIBA JESSICA ZAMEN · VALERIE STEELE · MELISSA SMITH
SHERRI MARIE GAUDET · JESSICA JANZEN OLSTAD · JORDAN PAIGE · STEPHANIE FOX
CAITLYN LAIRD · JANICE MEREDITH · NELI TAVARES HESSION · NAOMI HAUPT
LILA BEIJER · CANDICE RENEE BLIGHT · SHANNON-LEE FIGSBY · SUNIT SUCHDEV

You've Got This, Mama: A Mother's Guide To Embracing The Chaos And Living An Empowered Life
2018 Golden Brick Road Publishing House Inc. Trade Paperback Edition
Copyright @ 2018 Sabrina Greer

Published in Canada, for Global Distribution by Golden Brick Road Publishing House Inc.
www.goldenbrickroad.pub

For more information email: sabrina@ygtmama.com

ISBN
trade paperback: 978-1-988736-38-9
ebook: 978-1-988736-39-6
Kindle: 978-1-988736-40-2

To order additional copies of this book: orders@gbrph.ca

CONTENTS

INTRODUCTION

By Sabrina Greer

"You can allow fear
to take hold
or you can embrace
this beautiful chaos."

"There's no way to be a perfect mother
and a million ways to be a good one."
~ Jill Churchill

WHAT IS MOTHERHOOD? Have you ever thought about this question? I mean, seriously thought about it? The Oxford English dictionary defines motherhood as "the state or experience of having or raising a child." *Well, this is vague,* I thought to myself. So, I went on a quest to define motherhood on my terms. A well rounded, wholehearted, all-encompassing definition, relatable to all mothers. Let's be serious; motherhood is a helluva lot more than just having and raising a child, am I right?

In conducting my research (a lot of research), I concluded that it is impossible to have one blanket statement definition of motherhood because there are many variables, and every mother's journey is unique. Initially, I envisioned this book as what would be a collection of interviews. My one-sided view in all its glory, asking the mothers of the world what motherhood meant to them, then sharing their journeys. However, just as the germination of a tiny, microscopic cell (idea) becomes a fetus that grows through the miracle of pregnancy, it blossomed into something much grander and outside of my control.

While I could write an entire book on parenting, especially motherhood, it no longer felt like the task at hand. My new purpose was to be the vehicle that transported these diverse and empowering stories from so many brilliant moms to the needed ears of moms alike around the globe. While I have experienced many things within my intimate motherhood bubble, I realized that I have not even come close to experiencing all the things that can take place on this beautiful adventure. So rather than interpreting this magnificent data or attempting to recreate the voices of the people I was meeting, I decided instead to curate a collection of stories written and shared by the real mamas who experienced them.

Voila, the You've Got This, Mama, tribe is born. I am determined to bring together women from all walks of life, in all their differences with one commonality - motherhood. My life's new purpose is to build that infamous village we hear people tell us it takes to raise our children. To hand-pick the most fabulous variety of inspiring memoirs to share with you. In doing my due diligence, I've realized there is no other book like this out there. The millions of "how-to" parenting books and access to endless online resources can be overwhelming. We have instant access to a world of knowledge and "friends" at our immediate fingertips, yet we seem to be less prepared, more anxious, and more terrified than ever before. I like to refer to our generation of parents as the "Google Parent" meaning, if we have a question rather than consulting our said village, we go to the deep dark abyss called the world wide web. Don't get me wrong, while the internet is a valuable resource on many levels, it can also be a means to an end and fuel for that all too familiar mama-anxiety fire.

I wanted to learn more; this behavior fascinated me (call it my inner psych major). Another question I asked during interviews was this: "Why do moms default to the depths of the internet instead of consulting their physical tribe?" And a few more commonalities surfaced. Shame. Guilt. Fear. *Wait, what?* Moms are so ashamed to ask other moms for help because they: 1) Are too afraid of being judged for not having the tools to cope with a problem or, 2) Feel guilty for inconveniencing other mothers. Some even expressed that they were hesitant to speak to their own mother, step-mother, mother-in-law, or sister (immediate family) pertaining to parenting challenges. Where does this village mentality exist and how can I recreate it?

I want to create a safe place for mothers to get lost, even if for only a few moments. An environment for them to remember who they were while embracing who they have become. A place where judgment and shaming do not exist. There is no better comfort than knowing you're not alone and coming to terms with the fact that "you've got this!" We are not here to give advice or sell you the next "5-step" program to your desired outcome. We are not here to tell you when you should start solid food or that dairy is a no-no, how to sleep train your little one or when milestones should occur. We are a judgment-free, shame-free, guilt-free place where you can just be accepted and loved. This book is written by real moms, for real moms, from real mom life experiences.

Our village came together almost effortlessly; an *if you build it, they will come* scenario. I interviewed a diverse range of mothers to make sure we covered all the bases, and that we did. Guess what though? In our differences, our commonality has brought us together. Regardless of the career you held before becoming a mother or the career you are still juggling as a mother, irrespective of where you grew up, or how; whether you are a world traveler or if you never left the comfort of your city of origin; whether you have 20K+ followers on social media or have never heard of Facebook - **it does not matter**. If you are an entrepreneur, a brick/mortar business owner, a scholar, a teacher, a homemaker, a fitness instructor, or "just a mom." You are welcome here. Your race, your age, or your sexual orientation do not matter; if you are a mom, you are honored here. We are your tribe.

Motherhood comes with a lot of personal baggage (we know because we've got it too). It is not just changing diapers and cleaning house day in and day out. It is a never ending roller-coaster of emotions too. The internal guilt that comes with caring for another life - *Were those strawberries organic? What do I do, he's melting in the grocery store, again? Oh no, my baby rolled off the couch, should I take her to the hospital?* Then of course, the shame (seeing a theme here) and endless self-loathing which can be exaggerated by mommy groups and social media forums. I had a friend shamed right out of a mommy group for choosing to immunize her child. These emotions are typical and come with the territory of becoming a mom because motherhood is being everything to someone else. Motherhood is a continuous sacrifice - rewarded with giggles and cuddles. It is a full-time job with zero breaks and no pay, and is still beautiful, magical, and full of joy.

In my past life, I was many things and wore as many hats as I do today; just a different collection, a different season. I was an international model, a world traveler, a socialite, a free spirit, a hard worker, a student, a teacher, a daughter, a sister, and a friend, just to name a few. Today I am an entrepreneur, an author, a coach, a connector of inspiring souls, a lover of nature and all things beautiful, a voracious reader and lover of books, a dreamer, a doer, a wife, and my most important title of all is "mom." I am a mama to three incredible little boys. There is not one thing that defines me, yet a million things that make me who I am today. To me, motherhood means teaching another how to be the best version of themselves. Biology does not matter. How this person arrives into the world does not matter. What matters most is love - unconditional love and forgiveness, combined with a constant cycle of learning and growing. It means loving yourself first so you can teach your little ones how to be confident, independent, and secure while learning how to reciprocate love.

Motherhood is a gift, a miracle, a joyous celebration of life. However, it is also full of challenges and astronomical changes that aren't meant to be braved alone. We've got your back, mama. This book is a no bull, real deal, telltale collective, all about the beautiful chaos that is motherhood. No matter what stage you are at in your journey, what path you are following, or what mountain you are climbing, I am certain one of these divine souls will find their way to you. One, if not many, of these stories, will resonate and just might shine the light you need in the dark times. We want to teach you how to claim your power, embrace that chaos with grace and ease, and wear your cape like a boss, supermom! We want to empower you to live your best life regardless of how impossible that feels. You've got this, Mama!

Section 1

TRUSTING YOUR INSTINCTS AND PREPARING FOR THE UNEXPECTED

FEATURING
Sarah Secor-MacElroy
Jodie Tilley
Angela Muscat
Carrie Mazzei
Kristin Hallett

OPENING COMMENTARY BY
Sabrina Greer

I REMEMBER LOOKING IN the mirror at my twenty-nine-year-old self, thinking, *How did I get here?* I was in an emotionally abusive relationship, full of mistrust and infidelity, completely "settling" because my infamous "clock was ticking." *If not him, who? It's too late for me to find a baby-daddy now before my eggs dry up, I have already wasted so much time here, this will have to do.* What? I wanted to be a mom, sure. I also wanted my fairytale wedding, two-point-five kids, a white picket fence, and a golden retriever but at what expense?

It is incredible the pressure so many of us put upon ourselves, the ability we have to stand down and question our self-worth because we think we should be somewhere or someone we are not. I recently read Brené Brown's, *Braving The Wilderness.* This book is about the spiritual crisis society is experiencing with human disconnection, a quest to find true belonging. She writes, *"True belonging doesn't require you to change who you are; it requires you to be who you are."* Having the courage to BE who you truly are is when true joy will find you.

I became a mother to a beautiful, sweet, intelligent, quick-as-a-whip, six-year-old boy precisely one year after that mirror conversation with myself. My now hubby, the man of my dreams, brought me a ready-made, perfect little human and made me a stepmom. Exactly two years later, at thirty-two years of age, we made another one, together. Twenty-six months after that, our third son was born. I love my three children equally and am so grateful for every moment with them. Was this the picture perfect, Pinterest worthy plan I had envisioned as a young woman? Not verbatim. I wouldn't change a single freaking thing in hindsight. I am a massive advocate for living in the present moment, although, at times, I wonder *what would have been,* had I not broken free from the confines of my captured soul. I thank my lucky stars every day for that strength and courage I had just to be myself.

You see regardless of your belief system, whether it be God, the Universe, or some other Supreme Being, there is a plan. You do not need to share my belief in destiny or fate to be comforted and inspired by the idea that there is a greater design, a bigger picture that is out of our control. At times, even logic and reasoning won't explain why things unfold in a certain manner; you may even curse the very sky and stop believing in magic altogether, and that is okay. You are allowed to feel your emotions and trust me, honey, as a mama you will have feelings, lots of them. The only way to learn and grow is through them, when you explore them all.

My goal in writing this book was to share stories of the warriors that came before us, inspire mothers to surrender to what is out of their control. Empower you to live your best life and forget about the judgments and pressures of society through humor and sarcasm. This section would originally be named some hilariously, cheeky tagline intended to make you pee your pants (more so than you already are) however, very much like the book as a whole, it evolved and transformed into something much more significant right before my eyes. The stories in this book are powerful, transformative, and incredibly relatable. They won't make you want to pee, but I'm sure they will make you want to kick butt as a mom.

The commonality amongst the contributors in this section was a unity. Pregnancy is different for every mother. The psychology around becoming pregnant and coping with pregnancy - different. All the methods and experiences associated with pregnancy - different. The trials and tribulations throughout the process of creating a life - different. Globally, the labor and delivery methods, techniques, and experiences - astronomically different. So what is this unity I speak of? If every aspect and every layer are so unlike, what could join us?

Answer: The best plan is to abandon the plan!

That's right. The commonality uniting us is that things rarely go according to plan (at least our version of the plan). We put so much demand on everything being perfect, we forget to relax and enjoy the moments we are in. You may have heard these sayings before, "Once we stopped trying, we got pregnant immediately," or "As soon as I surrendered away from the rigid plan, everything worked out." You see, what resists, persists. Your thoughts are powerful. You may have heard the Napoleon Hill quote, *"What you think about, you bring about,"* right? If you spend all your time worrying and obsessing over what could go wrong, it might just go wrong.

I'm sure if you are experiencing morning sickness right now or reading this from your doctor prescribed bed rest, you are giving me the middle finger. I am not preaching or calling you overdramatic. Nor am I in any way belittling your unique experiences or suggesting you are a masochist who is purposely torturing yourself. I am merely encouraging you to surrender to the idea that some things might be out of your control and that is okay. I hope the stories in this section guide you to remove fear from the equation. To inhale love and exhale gratitude, even when you feel as though you cannot breathe at all. Trust that the path you are on is the path you are meant to be on and lean into it a little. Whatever you are going through, whatever stage you are at in your pregnancy or motherhood, I promise you, we promise you - **You've Got This, Mama!**

1

UNEXPECTED MOTHERHOOD

by Sarah Secor-MacElroy

"Beautiful things can grow from ugly, unwelcomed experiences."

Sarah Secor-MacElroy

Sarah Secor-MacElroy is a serial daydreamer with a gypsy soul. Over the past decade, Texas, Oregon, Czech Republic, Germany, and Montana have all been called home. She has always been resourceful and imaginative. From a young age she put pen to paper and soon realized she could materialize these daydreams with her tenacity, some ingenuity, and the occasional PowerPoint. Growing up, Sarah was shy and suffered from severe anxiety, always trying to seem aloof, she gained a reputation as the "bad girl." Sarah has always been impetuous, like the time she went to get her first tattoo and left with her entire back covered. She was later a reluctant debutante and college dropout, sinking back into anxiety and alcoholism. Eventually, Sarah found salvation in motherhood and again in the great outdoors. She found healing in hiking and cultivated a passion for wildlife conservation. Sarah is the Founder of, Mother of Wildthings, a blog which details life with her husband, Drew, and their three young sons. They are currently back in her hometown of Dallas, Texas for the free babysitting and to launch her latest venture, a sustainable children's clothing company, The Wild Life. Sarah's father is overjoyed that she is finally utilizing the Bachelor of Fine Arts Degree in Fashion and Retail Management he made her finish. Although she has spent a considerable amount of her adult life running from convention, she has found that putting down roots isn't the end of the adventures, but the beginning of opportunities she never imagined possible.

www.motherofwildthings.com
ig: @mother_of_wildthings
fb: amotherofwildthings

"You are in charge of how you react to the people and events in your life. You can either give negativity power over your life or you can choose happiness instead."
~ Anaïs Nin

SOMETIMES LIFE JUST HAPPENS, it feels as though it is happening at you and not to you; things don't play out like you had imagined or wished they would have. Unlike characters in made for tv movies, life doesn't fall into a perfect, predictable place every time. My passage into motherhood was entirely unintentional, and a huge surprise. My life had just spectacularly blown up in my face, and just a few months later, I was now facing the most serious endeavor of my life; ready or not, I was going to be someone's mom. Still picking up the pieces and trying to heal, I had to send a text message to a man I had known for precisely three months, and let him know he was going to be a dad. We lived in two different countries and had been on only three dates when I sent that text. And believe it or not, six months earlier, had been my grand fairytale wedding to another man. Immediately following the wedding, we moved across the country from Texas to Oregon, full of hope for our future. A few weeks into our marriage, I discovered that we were, in fact, not legally married. He was still married to his "ex-wife," and throughout our relationship, he had been hooking up with anyone who would swipe right on his online profiles. Hurt, humiliated, and lost, I packed up my dog and what little else I cared for, and flew home.

Going home just magnified my despair. Still broken and dejected, I would hang out at local bars to forget my troubles, but inevitably,

I would always run into someone who would ask why I was back so soon or worse, cock their head to the side and give me the "bless your heart" look that everyone in the world seems to give and say, "I heard what happened..." I packed my bags again, sent my dog to my mom's house and took off for a country I knew almost nothing about. I was riding high on my journey of self-discovery and newfound independence when I met a man in a moment of serendipity, and we were thrust into the adventure of becoming parents and partners when we barely knew each other. I had gone from a heartbroken girl to self-confident woman to pregnant immigrant in the span of half a year. None of this is how I would have planned it (had that been an option). Thankfully, the Universe didn't consult me. These experiences, both pleasant and unpleasant, led me to become the woman I am today; a mother of three sons, an entrepreneur and writer, and the mother they *need*. Often, I hear women saying that they will be ready to be a mom when x and y align or when life falls entirely into place. The journey into the unknown, although sometimes riddled with snares and setbacks, can lead to the most magical possibilities.

Many of us have fallen into the trap of believing we have to be perfectly put together adults before we can become good parents. I'm growing up along with my firstborn. The woman I am today is someone I never thought I would be or even could be. I was a wild child, a party girl who couldn't even keep my French bulldog alive without my mom having joint custody. I was still making some interesting and questionable choices until the day I saw "pregnant" appear on that little screen. I took many, many pregnancy tests and it took almost a week for this new reality to finally sink in. Once I had a grasp(ish) on what was happening, I had to tell the dad. We lived a few hours apart, and he spent a lot of time traveling for his job, so I had days to mull over what I was going to do, and I came up with two plans. One for if he was angry and wanted nothing to do with us, and another for if he was as excited and happy as I was. I still have the text message saved as a picture on my desktop computer: "I didn't want to send this in a text, but I just can't wait another two weeks to tell you... I'm sorry, I love you, oops and congratulations, you're going to be a dad." My other option was a half-baked plan to go live in Sweden, which would have never worked out. Thankfully, he was all in, and I didn't have to emigrate again. People around me were fairly shocked when they found out I was expecting just a few months after my life imploded. It was the last thing anyone, including myself, expected. My husband, then baby-daddy, and I were both told we were not ready; comments ranged from encouraging to downright disparaging, one person even suggested we put the baby up for adoption. I thought it would be easy to ignore the naysayers from two thousand miles away, but pregnancy hormones are not very forgiving. It is not easy to forge on when it feels like everyone doubts you. Your past might feel as though a weight is hanging from your neck, and people may continue to judge you based on attitudes and decisions you feel were made a lifetime ago. Always remember that your past does not define you. Your future can be limitless if you can rise above the negative voices and naysayers. Never allow anyone to make you feel bad about who you used to be. I won't say it happens frequently, but occasionally, I will run into an old acquaintance who is surprised to find out that the shy, anxious, co-dependent lush they once drank with is now a happily married and well-adjusted member of society. A decade ago, nobody would have guessed that this is the path my life would take. I dated jerks, losers, and abusers; I suffered from low self-esteem and anxiety, so much so, that I dropped out of university the first time around because my fear of talking to other people was practically paralyzing. Being thrown head first into motherhood forced me to grow up and adapt quickly. It didn't happen overnight, and it was hard work to change, but I started by immediately shedding what vices I could; smoking and drinking were the first to go.

Over the next nine months, I let go of old wounds and pain I had long held onto. I also worked on learning how to forgive, let go of fear, anger, and narcissism. I had to find a way to mitigate, what one of my dear friends kindly calls my flakiness, my gypsy soul. I couldn't be a stable mother and always be on the move, running away from conventionality. Anxiety and doubt is a natural occurrence, particularly when you are dealing with the unknown. I had zero experience with children, let alone babies. The last time I had been near a baby, I was six years old, and my youngest cousin had just been born. Since I hung out mostly in bars, and I had no friends with kids, I felt lost in the beginning. I began reading any and every book I could get my hands on about motherhood, pregnancy, and childbirth; I learned about tiger mothers, free-range parents, helicopter moms, natural birth, elective c-sections, breast pumps, and everything in between. I imagined what kind of mother I wanted to be, and envisioned the life I wanted to provide for the little person growing inside of me. My anxiety transformed into determination and courage. All I knew is that I never wanted my child to feel the way I did while I was growing up - I had a voice, but when I wanted to use it, no sound came out. Anxiety feels as though you are confined, and your thoughts and ideas can't make their way out. It can come across as though you are aloof or uninterested in the people and things around you. I found the books about natural childbirth empowering and read, and reread, Ina May's, *Guide to Childbirth* and *Hypnobirthing*. I found a doula and natural birthing center that looked to be straight out of a dream; it wasn't in the least bit intimidating or clinical. I was determined to have a magical birthing experience; I wanted to have a water birth, and put all my mental and physical energy into preparing for it. At thirty-nine weeks, my baby was still stubbornly breech, he had set up shop and not moved from that position for weeks. Evidently, he would not budge, and I had to let go of my perfectly planned, idealized birth, and settle for a very scary and clinical c-section. I felt like a failure, and I felt as though I had been cheated.

From this experience and many more to come, I learned that it is okay to lament what could have been. It is okay to be upset when something doesn't go the way you planned, but be careful and do not linger there too long. The genesis of my first child and his birth taught me the valuable lesson - expect the unexpected. Understanding this has served me well as my life continues to take an unexpected trajectory most of the time. I wrongly assumed I would easily conceive the second time around, never dreaming it will involve three years, several miscarriages, a team of doctors, surgery, and assisted reproduction technology. I did not plan on my husband's military career ending abruptly and him becoming a disabled veteran. Trudging silently through my personal infertility hell, and suddenly in need of a job after years of being a stay at home mom, I didn't think things could get any worse. But, they did. We were dealt the blow of our oldest son being diagnosed with autism, and it would take years of testing, tears, speech therapy, and stress before finding out that this was an incorrect diagnosis. With everything going wrong in my life again, it would have been easy to sink into depression and despair. Choosing to see the bright side or be joyful when it felt like the world was disintegrating beneath me wasn't always easy. However, wisdom sometimes comes from peculiar places such as a song. On our trip home from speech therapy with my son, I heard The Grateful Dead's, *Scarlet Begonias*, and the words just struck me and have stuck with me ever since, *"Once in a while you get shown the light in the strangest of places if you look at it right."* My husband leaving the military opened the door to us having the freedom to move anywhere we wanted to go. That decision guided us to live in a place with excellent healthcare and to the insightful team of doctors that diagnosed a congenital defect in my uterus. That birth defect was the reason my first child was so stubbornly breech and why I had remained unsuccessful in conceiving a second child for all those years. These experiences came to fruition because some guy cheated on me and annihilated my heart.

My adverse experiences became positive ones, once I finally conceived my twins. However, my pregnancy with them was awful. It is hard to reconcile something so awe-inspiring and incredible such as conceiving after years of being unable to, then having the experience itself be nightmarish. Each trimester brought its own set of challenges, and more emergency labor and delivery visits than I can count. By twenty weeks, I firmly held onto the singular hope that I could keep them in for just ten more weeks. I made it ten more weeks, and then another three, and at thirty-three weeks, I felt the dreadful, but all too familiar feeling of blood welling. Twenty minutes to midnight, I wept as nurses prepared me for surgery, trembling and afraid for my babies, I fell asleep as they began the surgery. I awoke, no longer pregnant in a dimly lit recovery room. I hadn't even seen a glimpse of their faces, let alone embrace them, and have skin to skin contact; they were whisked off to the neonatal intensive care unit (NICU) just as quickly as they were born. They spent the next few weeks in the NICU; their tiny bodies riddled with tubes and cords hooked up to beeping machines. It is gut-wrenching to have a life you just created taken away and hooked up to machines, but even in this bleak time, I sought the light. I plugged into an online community for parents experiencing the same things I was - the trials and tribulations of the NICU, and found strength in our shared experiences. I did not get the pregnancy or delivery I wanted, there were no beautiful photos of my sons being born, the hospital mixed up their names on the birth certificates, and I languished for what felt like forever on bedrest, missing out on my older child's life; the negativity dragged me down, but once again, I focused on finding the light. This adverse experience was the springboard for me to start a business I had dreamed of since I was a little girl. An opportunity I never knew existed, all because I had babies almost two months too soon. I quickly learned about the lack of preemie clothing readily available, and this laid the foundation for starting a children's clothing line.

My message in all is this: **Never lose hope and try as hard as you can to look for the glimmer of light in the darkness.** It may only be a tiny speck of light, but I promise you, it is there. Beautiful things can grow from ugly, unwelcomed experiences. My three sons have become the driving force in my life to achieve and be more. At the end of my life, regardless of anything I do, they will be my greatest accomplishment. They are the catalysts that made me let go of my past and realize that I am enough. Every fiber of my being changed when I took my first-born son home from the hospital. At first, I was beyond scared. The amount of information out there for a first-time mom is vast and overwhelming. I slowly found my path and my ethos as a mother. As I became more confident in my new role of mom, that confidence overflowed into other areas of my life. My energy, my goals, and entire capacity as a human being shifted by creating these tiny people. Motherhood has been so empowering for me, it helped me find my voice and my passion. As Arthur Golden said in *Memoirs of a Geisha*, "*Adversity is like a strong wind. It tears away from us all but the things that cannot be torn, so that we see ourselves as we really are.*" We have to let go of the anxiety, the feelings of not being enough, and the guilt that stems from not being able to be everything to everyone in our lives. I am here to tell you that no matter where you are in life, you can be everything that your child needs. If you are reading this, and have found yourself to be pregnant by surprise, do not waste your time agonizing over what anyone else thinks. I know it's hard, and sometimes it will hurt, but you have to power through. If you aren't where you want to be, envision the future you want and build it for yourself and your child, moment by moment, and brick by brick. Embrace the journey ahead of you. You can be a student and a mom; an entrepreneur and a mom; a CEO and a mom; a work in progress and a mom, or even a combination of these. You have to decide to go after whatever you desire and remember that you do not have to have everything completely figured out. Don't allow fear to hold you hostage. Strive to better yourself every day, not only for your child and family, but also for yourself. Dream big, set goals, try new things, dye your hair, move to a far-flung place if that's your vision, just do not settle for a life that is less than what you deserve. Ready or not; expected or unexpected - we have all embarked on the same mission. No matter what your journey into motherhood looks like, whether you made a tiny human or opened your heart up to care for someone else's greatest creation, you are now a part of a club. This club isn't exclusive, and the perks aren't particularly glamorous, but you are part of a global community that is powerful and supportive. We have the greatest, scariest, most tiring, and trying job there is, but we are all on the most wonderful and impactful journey of all.

~ To my sons, Sterling, Hunter and Gavin
and the fingerprints you all have left on my heart.
I love you more than you will ever know.

2

DESTINY
VS. DETERMINATION

by Jodie Tilley

"Trust your journey, trust your timing and let your destiny reveal itself."

Jodie Tilley

Born with the sand between her toes, this Aussie beach bum now calls Canada, home. Having grown up on the eastern shores of Oz, the Aussie culture runs deeply through her veins. Spending the second half of her life in the Canadian wild west, she is now just as comfortable donning her cowgirl boots as she is when riding the waves at her favo-favoriterite childhood beach.

Jodie spent her childhood watching her father compete in swimming, triathlons, and surf lifesaving carnivals, so it's no surprise she also has a few medals lying around, including her most proud medals from the Boston Marathon and her half Ironman. But when asked what her greatest achievement is, she beams as she proclaims that it's being a mother to her twin boys. She spent two relentless decades waiting to meet them, but they had their own plan for when they would make their debut. This was when Jodie learned her greatest lesson - to trust in the journey.

Jodie will also tell you that one of her purposes in this life is to be a connector. She is responsible for twelve of her friends' weddings and receives enormous joy from being able to facilitate other's happiness. This would also explain why her labor of love is newborn photography, and why she thrives in her new entrepreneurial endeavor as owner and founder of PHI Medical Aesthetics- a business that restores confidence in women by helping to beautyPHI, and restore their youth.

www.beautyPHI.com
ig: @Beauty_PHI
fb: Beauty PHI Medical Aesthetics

"We cannot control the wind, but we can adjust the sails."
~ Thomas S. Monson

ESTINY... I WASN'T sure I even believed in the concept. It seemed like such a cliché when people would say, "It's your destiny." However, reaching mommyhood status two months shy of age forty-two, I now believe while we all have a destiny of sorts, we also create our own path. Let's jump back about a century ago... in England, on a sunny day in March, 1916, a pregnant woman late in her third trimester was riding a horse as this was a standard mode of transportation back then. That fateful day, a horrible tragedy took place, the horse got spooked and tossed her to the ground, then trampled on her torso. She went into labor immediately and delivered not one, but two baby girls that day - one alive and one dead. To this day, I thank every God out there and all the higher powers that be, that the baby twin born alive, kicking, and screaming, was my grandmother! And so my destiny begins...

Twins, They're In My Bloodline

My grandmother's older sister was pregnant six times and birthed nine living children! (Quick, do the math!) That means she had three sets of TWINS! Which means I have three sets of second cousin twins, or cousins once removed or whatever title you want to give it. The truth is, I have never met any of them, so growing up, twins weren't at the forefront of my mind. And as my grandmother's fraternal twin sister died in utero, the hereditary gene that passed down the line never resonated with me. Nevertheless, as a child, teenager, and adult, I became obsessed with TWINS!

Is it any surprise that in my late teens and then in my thirties, I dated three sets of twins? Yep, I know what you're thinking, and naturally, it begs the question. So listen, the first two sets of twins were identical. I can't help that I got them mixed up in the dark one night (or two)! Thankfully, the third time around, I moved onto fraternal twins who had a height difference of about a foot and weight difference of approximately one hundred pounds. Fortunately for me, no more innocent mix-ups in the dark!

Not only did I have this obsession with twins, but I was born with this inherent desire to mother every baby I could get my hands on. Pre cabbage patch hysteria, I had a baby-that-away doll, and a Baby Alive doll, and I made those my own twin babies. I would hold them to my three-year-old bosom and try to feed them. I would change their wet diapers... yes Baby Alive dolls pee their pants! I would push them around in a stroller, read to them in my rocking chair, and put them to sleep at night in their cribs. I was a proud mother and thought I was doing a damn good job (as a three-year-old).

Ah, The Joys Of Young Love

It turns out this wasn't a little girl phase, the desire and drive to be a mother grew into my teens and twenties. At the mature and all-knowing age of twenty, I had a serious boyfriend (an identical TWIN). We had been together three years already and had spent the prior two planning our whole lives together as young loves do. We had chosen our future golden retriever's name, and names for each of our three perfect children who would be born at two-year intervals. I remember asking my mother if I could book her for New Year's Eve, 1999 to babysit my THREE kids! It was 1993 at the time.

So, when I found myself single after four years together, and this dream shattered, off I journeyed to the Great White North to have some fun, my right as a twenty-one-year-old! That year abroad passed so quickly and I wasn't ready to leave. I was having the time of my life, I was in love again and already planning my next family (in my head). Little did I know, I had come across my first serial cheater. And by serial

I mean I learned of thirteen women he had been with during our time together, and those are just the ones I found out about. Thank goodness for good friends who couldn't stand by and watch me be fooled into loving a man who didn't know how to love me back.

Years of heartbreaks (plural) ensued (interject nice guy here and there), and my family was desperate to convince me to return home so they could nurture my broken heart. Oblivious to the lesson I was meant to learn, I persevered and continued to look for love in all the wrong places.

Fast forward a few years later, I was twenty-nine and living in Halifax, and I had a friend who was about to turn thirty-five. She desperately wanted to be a mother but had not found a suitable willing participant in her life plan. I remember hearing defeat in her story as she felt like she had lost her chance. That night, I made a pact with myself (I even wrote and signed a contract to hold myself accountable), that if I were still single by the time I turned thirty-five, I would find myself a donor (of the sperm kind) and fulfill my destiny to become a mother. I started researching the type of designer sperm donor that one could choose. That part was exciting!

Here Comes The Bride (Almost)

A month after I signed my single motherhood contract with myself, I met the man of my dreams (or so I thought). He was my everything, and I, his. Life was grand, exciting, full of adventures and dreams with him. After living together in Halifax for a few years, we moved to Western Canada to explore new opportunities; I bought us a house, we traveled, we got engaged, and we planned our wedding and our family. Life was splendid for a while. Although we both loved each other intensely, we still went through a rollercoaster of experiences during the five years we were together. There were even times when we would go to the brink of breakup. We developed an unhealthy codependency, and neither of us had the strength to leave at the time or the will to be without each other. So the rollercoaster continued.

However, while planning our wedding, I had absolutely no idea of the sheer devastation that awaited me. He was falling out of love with me and in love with another. She was his escape. I was a constant reminder of the rules that were needed for our relationship to survive. She was not. Based on my own fears of losing him, I tried to control and mother him. She did not. He was increasing his athletic training schedule to spend more time with her, and less time with me. In retrospect, the red flags were there, but I chose to ignore them. My destiny was within my grasp, and I wasn't about to let anything or anyone get in my way! We stopped using contraception three months before our wedding day, hopeful of an immediate conception. His anxiety grew and manifested physically. One day, I came home from work to find him curled up on the floor in the fetal position, hyperventilating. He was afraid and incapable of sharing his truth. I continued to convince myself he had "cold feet," and that we would be fine if we could just get to the damn altar. Fortunately (I can say that now), he found the strength to leave me stranded at the altar (not actually at the altar, it was days before). The details of my life for the next few months were foggy. I was now the one curled up in the fetal position just trying to breathe. This destroyed me! *How could life ever be the same without him?* I only knew myself as the other half of him. I lost a huge part myself that day, and once again my destiny was brought into question. It truly was the "dark year" of my life. My dreams fell apart, and as he moved on with his life with another, it seemed there was nothing I could do to bring them back. I feared a life without him and was worried I might never find that kind of love again. I feared I didn't have enough time to heal and find a partner who I could have a family with, and I feared failure, again!

True to my contract of six years prior, off I marched to the fertility clinic to discuss my options, terrified that my stupid contract had become my reality. I was about to turn thirty-five and feared, the often thrown in your face, statistics of aging eggs and loss of fertility after age thirty-five. However, I was determined NOT to give up on my "destiny" of becoming a mother. I grew serious about it and began my fertility testing. Once again, I researched the sperm banks to create my designer baby.

The Baby That Wasn't Meant To Be

Still mending a broken heart, I wasn't entirely ready to pull the plug and become an impregnated single mum. So I convinced myself that harvesting, fertilizing, and freezing my eggs so that they were ready and waiting was a good plan B to have in place. About a month away from pulling the trigger on buying my designer sperm, destiny knocked on my front door again... literally. This time, in the form of a tall, six-foot-two-inches, green-eyed, dirty-blonde, brilliant, ambitious, athletic, successful, salt of the earth, kind and authentic Prairie boy! And... he was a TWIN! Mr. Perfect and I developed an intense mutual adoration for each other. All that previous heartache suddenly seemed purposeful. We moved fast! Three months into dating each other, we moved in together (my modus operandi). *What sperm bank?* We began planning our future, talking about having children, and booking our world travels which we had to get in before my eggs expired. He was entirely on board (or was he?). We were madly in love, but the voice inside kept wondering if it was too good to be true.

He was much younger than I but seemed much more mature than his age. We decided we would start our family about a year into our relationship. Assuming it might take a while given my age, and that it didn't happen the first time I tried for several consecutive months in a previous relationship, we decided we could eliminate contraception. About nine months into our coupling, and without trying, we fell pregnant! Albeit shocked and a few months sooner than we had planned, I couldn't have been happier.

My early pregnancy symptoms were intense. But having never been pregnant before, I had nothing to compare it to. I experienced all the typical early symptoms but also had severe stabbing and cramping sensations at times. Thinking this was "normal," I persevered through the rough nights. We had already planned a month-long trip to Europe before learning about the pregnancy, so my doctor suggested an early ultrasound before we left to reassure us of a healthy baby. It was scheduled for the day before our flight. The morning of the ultrasound, I got up and went for a run, I had been feeling much better than the few weeks prior. We drove to the ultrasound clinic full of excitement. I lay on the bed with my uncomfortably full bladder and awaited the view of the little beating heart on the monitor. The technician didn't seem too sure of herself and asked us to stay put so that the doctor could speak with us. It was that moment I began to tremble. I knew, by her reaction and lack of response when I questioned if everything was okay with the baby, something was wrong. The doctor came in and confirmed the sad news. I had an ectopic pregnancy which meant the eleven-week fetus had ruptured my fallopian tube. All that was going through my mind was that we HAD to save the baby, and there MUST be a way to re-implant the fetus into my uterus. But the doctor's concern in that moment was to save MY life. I was bleeding into my abdomen; she estimated that I had acclimated about 300ml of pooling blood in my abdominal cavity. She ordered us to go directly to the hospital for emergency surgery. I was devastated by the news of being told I was about to lose the baby that was still living inside me. How could I have such bad luck? However, had I stepped onto that plane to France the next morning, I would not have walked off the plane alive.

The ectopic pregnancy robbed me of not only my baby, but also half of my reproductive organs. There was no saving my right fallopian tube. It was irreparable, and they had to remove it along with the tennis ball sized fetus. As my body recovered, my hormones and emotional stability went haywire. I was mourning the loss of the next fifty years that I had spent the last two months planning. I couldn't see a pregnant belly without bursting into hysterics. *That was my chance! I was thirty-six years old and eleven weeks pregnant. Why did this happen to me?* I was obsessed with trying again immediately. It was my sole focus. Over the next couple of months, I lost sight of what my partner wanted, and I acted like it was my right, and that we needed to put all focus on becoming pregnant again. This time though with the additional challenge of working with only half of my reproductive system.

My obsession with wanting to try again soon after, highlighted a disconnect between what my partner and I wanted. He was spooked and emotional, but mature enough to realize that he wasn't ready to go there again so soon. This process had shown him he needed more time to prepare for fatherhood, and that we didn't share the same timelines and pressure to reach parenthood. Isn't that the most unfair difference between a man and a woman? Our damn biological clocks and our obsession with them often results in the breakdown of a once well-matched relationship.

This breakup crippled me! I'd lost the man I loved and a baby. At the time, it felt even harder than being left at the altar. And, I was now three years older. Approaching thirty-seven, I felt the pressure to buy the designer sperm, harvest my eggs, and implant them. Meanwhile, on the other side of the world, my younger sister and her wife had been making plans to start a family of their own. My sister had become pregnant to a turkey baster! Yep, Williams Sonoma could launch a whole new Thanksgiving marketing campaign! My beautiful niece who was born nine months later is living proof that this doesn't just happen in the movies. So this got me thinking, maybe I didn't need to spend thousands of dollars on a designer baby... perhaps I could approach some of my single guy friends that would want to help a friend in need and just give me, oh I dunno, 80,000,000 or so of their little swimmers and I too could put them inside a turkey baster and impregnate myself? And so began my new mission.

Against Better Judgement

Just to kill some time, I agreed to be set up. Apparently, living the single life wasn't my strong suit. Enter serial cheater number two! *Man, did I LOVE the bad boys.* Six months into dating, he received a job transfer out East. Due to some early warning signs, my gut was telling me to end it but he insisted on doing long distance, and against my better judgement, my one lonesome ovary won the battle and I capitulated to his wishes. Over the course of the next two years, we saw each other regularly and had some fantastic times together. I loved him desperately and continued to ignore every red flag being waved in my direction. Desperate for a child, I somehow convinced him to enroll in the fertility clinic to begin our individual fertility testing.

Whilst we were on vacation with my family in Australia, and in a dramatic scene in front of four family members around the breakfast table, I made the shattering discovery of his two month long relationship with the "girlfriend" in Florida. When she called his phone and I answered, she was as shocked as I was to learn that there was another woman in his life to which he had promised the world. That feeling of betrayal by someone you thought you loved with every ounce of yourself has got to be one of the most debilitating and crushing feelings in the world.

Stupidly, I let him convince me to give him another chance. Clearly I wasn't coming from a place of strength at the time. A couple of months later I flew to surprise him for the weekend. When I arrived, all my Spidey senses were tingling. I stole his phone, locked myself in the bathroom (as you do) and my world crumbled again. My suspicion that I couldn't trust him was confirmed and validated by the discovery of multiple women with whom he was cavorting or engaging in affairs with. Some were long term, some were new, some were in the making. That day was a painful but final goodbye.

I was now forty! *Was it too late?* I felt incredibly stupid for not following through with my contract. *How did I expect my forty-year-old eggs to have any life left in them?* I was so angry at myself, at the men who wasted my time because they were lying, cheating sociopaths, at the good guys who didn't cheat but just stalled my progression to motherhood, at the world for leaving me alone and with no family to call my own! So I decided that I had one last kick at this can and headed back to the fertility specialist. What were the statistics for me now over forty? If I had any chance above zero, I was going for it! I revisited the turkey baster scenario, I talked with three guy friends who all had great qualities and would make excellent donors! To my surprise, all three volunteered to help. Only one of them made it conditional on assisting in the "traditional" method for conception. So after a few months of deliberation, I made my decision. I decided on the perfect donor, and off I went to Williams Sonoma!

Destiny Interrupted My Plans With The Turkey Baster

I set myself a new timeline - January, 2015, my sperm donor, the turkey baster, and I had a hot date! I was already planning the scene complete with cranberry scented candles, a satin robe and Vance Joy playing softly in the background. But it was summertime, and I was all about the live music and hanging out with friends. If my conception plan came to fruition, then I certainly wouldn't be partying like a rockstar for the next couple of years, or ever. So one last summer of Jodie it was. One hot summer serendipitous night, sixteen friends and I had planned to hit a Broken Bells concert in Calgary. I'd just seen them three days prior in Chicago, and I had to be in Toronto the next morning for 8am meetings, but the whispers told me, *Just go, and suck up the red-eye flight.* Earlier that day one of the sixteen friends had fallen ill and offered up her ticket, another girlfriend spoke up and claimed it for her husband's cousin. Hmm, a mystery man - fresh meat!

I met my friends across the road at a bar for a pre-concert drink. There he was, the fresh meat. Not only did he look fresh, but he also looked quite young. With the help of six years of Botox, the eight-year age gap was indiscernible. He immediately intrigued me, and "coincidentally" we ended up sitting beside each other at the show.

A week later, we had our first date! It was one for the books, and let's just say it involved an Aussie DJ, lots of vodka, slip & slide on an olive oiled counter, hide and seek around his parents house (he was house sitting while they were away), naked bodies in a hot tub, lots of puke (mine, I blame the heat from the hot tub), and there's a vague memory of him wearing my lingerie while giving me a lap dance, but NO sex! Our second date involved chocolate body paint for dessert and NO sex... the hot and spontaneous yet sexless fun dates continued like this for some time! I highly recommend this strategy ladies!

On our fourth date, I told him I didn't want to scare him away, but I was preparing to become a single mother in the new year. I made it very clear he better not get in my way and that we should not get too involved. We planned on ending our relationship by Christmas if we were still seeing each other. But little did I know, destiny had a different plan for me!

I approached this relationship very differently. For the first time in my life, I stopped trying to force something to feel right. I quit pressurizing the guy to get to a place to agree to have children with me. And in letting go, the most beautiful thing happened. I allowed life to unfold and it evolved into something wonderful! For the first time, I trusted the outcome. I didn't need him to fulfill my destiny. To my absolute surprise, three months into dating he told me he was in love with me and wanted to be a part of my plan to start a family, and on MY timeline! *WTF? No! That's not what thirty-three-year-old guys do! They play the field, and they spread their seed!* But this one was different; he wanted IN! He wanted ME! And a lifetime together! Even knowing the likelihood that this would be a long and expensive process, he signed up for ALL OF IT! It was fast, but for once, it just felt right. So, we pulled the goalie, not expecting a miracle, but just a month later, unexpected symptoms suggested that we pee on a stick. And there it was, that much anticipated clear blue line. I couldn't believe it! *We tried only ONCE! I've tried for two decades and failed with others, how could it be this easy this time?* As excited as I was, I knew all too well that statistics would not be in my favor to grow, carry, and deliver a healthy baby.

With my history of an ectopic pregnancy, my doctor wanted an early ultrasound. The day arrived, and as I lay on the treatment bed in the ultrasound room, I began sweating profusely. I was terrified that just like every other time in my life when the carrot was dangled, it would be ripped away from me. I fully expected to learn that day it was another ectopic pregnancy taking place in my one remaining fallopian tube, or that there was no heartbeat. As the ultrasound technician panned over to my right and found what she was looking for, she turned the monitor to us and proclaimed, "Congratulations! There's your baby's heartbeat!" There it was, something resembling a pea was flickering on the screen! It was a teeny tiny heartbeat, but we could see the embryo clearly. She said the heartbeat was strong and the embryo was exactly where it needed to be. A glimpse of motherhood was in my sights! As we were both soaking in the happy news, the technician panned over to the other side of my uterus, zoomed in and announced, "And here we have your other baby's heartbeat! You're having TWINS!" Did she say TWINS?! DESTINY, WE DID IT!

Motherhood Arrives And Lessons Learned

The eight months that followed were terrifying at times, exhausting, exciting, and hormonally charged. However, after fifty-four hours of torturous labor, culminating in an emergency c-section, my perfect healthy twin boys finally arrived! But they weren't the only ones born that day. A mother was also born. And in those first moments, while holding our babies, my greatest lesson was realized - my whole life, until I met the father of my babies, I tried to force my own dreams, hopes, and expectations to be a mother on my respective partners. I tried to control and steer my relationships towards parenthood. And when I felt scared or like I was losing control, I micromanaged even more. At those times, I felt batshit crazy and didn't like the person I was. When all I ever needed to do was trust my journey, trust my timing, and trust my destiny. My two little souls were always out there, just waiting for their mama to be ready to learn her greatest lesson.

> ~ To my twin sons, my world, my universe, my EVERYTHING! You bring me immeasurable joy. Thank you for teaching me about trust and patience. To say you were worth the wait is a major understatement. To my husband, for embracing the challenge of twin parenthood with maturity and grace and more courage than I had myself.

3

WHEN PLAN A BECOMES PLAN C

by Angela Muscat

"*Trust your motherly instincts; they are always right*"

Angela Muscat

Angela was born and raised in Toronto, Ontario, Canada. She is a often described as a kind, loving, helpful, and loyal woman - traits which were nurtured and cultivated by taking care of her mother who had bipolar disorder and two awesome younger brothers. First, Angela's post-secondary direction took her towards law, however she found her passion in police foundations. She completed her diploma and soon realized she loved being with, and helping children, likely inspired by the sixteen year age gap with her youngest sibling. She went back to school to become a registered early childhood educator (RECE). One of Angela's biggest goals in life was to write a book; a dream which is being realized. She is excited to be a part of this coauthoring journey and share her experiences on her greatest accomplishment yet, becoming a mother. Angela loves to travel but her favorite time is that spent with her family. She is a wife to Arynn and a mother to her one-year-old babe, Tyson.

ig: @angielala11

"A mother's instincts are worth more than a medical degree."
~ Dr. Susan Markel

ON THURSDAY, JANUARY 5th, 2017 AT 8:47PM, our lives changed forever. As I lay on a silver operating table, I looked over at my husband (who was white in the face and in complete shock) and asked, "Is he okay? He is not crying!" My husband then responded, "Yes, he is okay." I looked towards the ceiling and sighed with relief. I was so nervous as I had no idea what was going on around me and couldn't see anything. Well, I could, it was a large blue sheet right in front of my face. My legs and stomach were numb, and I felt excited, scared, nervous, and helpless. I never knew I could feel so many emotions all at once. Then, they showed him to me. Finally, after ten long months, I got to see his face. And he was just so beautiful. Perfect. Exactly everything that I had hoped for and dreamed of. "He is so cute," I said to the nurse. Our son, Tyson, was then handed over to my husband for skin to skin contact while I lay there, cold and shaking, thinking, *What now?* They put a hot blanket on me, *Boy does it ever feel good,* and told me I would have to wait one hour in the recovery room.

So, as you guessed, I had a c-section. I thought I would be the first one to hold my son. It was not like that. I remember the doctor saying to me, "You made the best decision for your son by having a c-section. The umbilical cord was wrapped around his neck." It is so scary to think things like this happen. Now it makes sense why he was not crying at birth. Thank God everything was okay. I was so relieved when the doctor had told me this, but, why did I feel so let down? In our society, when we divulge that we had a c-section everyone asks, "Well why?" "What happened?" "Was that your only option?" If this is the safest option for you and your baby, then do it! Stop worrying about the judgments and do you, Mama!

My husband and I had less than twelve hours to decide if we should have a c-section or not. I was forty-one weeks and four days pregnant when I gave birth. To put this into perspective, this was nearly TEN months. Our little man just did not want to come out. I tell you if he could stay in there forever I think he would have. Well, this is how I felt at the time. I was at the point of shouting "Get this baby out of me!" My midwife sent me to the hospital to get an ultrasound on Wednesday to see what was going on in there. The doctor that took the ultrasound said, "Well, it looks like you have a big baby! Nine pounds and thirteen ounces!" "What?" I say. This is not something that a first-time mom wants to hear!

Oh man, now that's a big baby, and there is only one way out! I kept thinking. Then the doctor said, "Your options are, a) A vaginal birth, but you should know there could be complications as he is a big baby. He could break his shoulder when coming out, the cord could be wrapped around his neck, or option b) You could have a cesarean section which of course could have potential complications as well. You could get an infection, have heavy blood loss, or bowel problems. I can't tell you what to do; this is something that the two of you need to decide. I can tell you that this baby needs to come out by Friday at the latest. So I will let your midwife know." I look at my husband and think here we are, our first big decision as parents. We have to decide by tonight and see the midwife tomorrow morning to let her know our decision.

As we racked our brains that night trying to figure out what was best for our son, we decided on a c-section. *A C-SECTION?* For the past ten months, having a c-section was not even on my mind. I never thought this could happen to me. Even after being pregnant for what felt like forever, I questioned everything. *Was this the right move? Should I have gone with an obstetrician? Would they have let my pregnancy go on this long? My midwives said they would induce me if needed, and it was, because Tyson's head was not engaging, but we never talked about a c-section.* I did not prepare myself at all and was in shock that I would be walking into the hospital tomorrow with no contractions, no labor pains, hospital bag packed, and my husband right there next to me. I would not be screaming my husband's name due to the worst pain of my life. There would be no water breaking. I pictured my birth process would be just like how it was in the movies. My water would break, we would rush to the hospital, while I had contractions in the car. *Maybe, I would have the baby in the car?* Okay, I know, I did not want that to happen, but you never know. These are the thoughts that run through your head.

After I had Tyson, I started talking to other moms and non-moms and realized that there were a lot of people out there, like myself who had no education around c-sections. Then I thought, *I want to educate women and men about this so they don't have to be alone.* Yes, even men, all men, not just the fathers, need to understand what is going on so they can help. I had people ask me, "Did you bleed after you had a c-section?" Some even said, "Oh I know why you had one, it's because your hips were not big enough." Yes, you do bleed. So make sure you have lots of pads in that baby bag. It doesn't matter if your hips are big or not, if you need a c-section, then you need a c-section, and there is nothing wrong with that.

This led me to want to debunk the myths around c-sections. I started my research and came across an article in the magazine *Reader's Digest* titled, *7 C-Section Myths Pregnant Women Should Know,* by Julia Haskins, which did just that. Julia talks about the first myth being, "If you have a c-section, you won't be able to enjoy skin to skin contact with your baby." She says, "While certain parts of your body may be more sensitive to the touch following a c-section, there's no reason that the procedure should get in the way of skin to skin contact between you and your baby. It may just take some time to find a position that is comfortable for you." This is true, even though I didn't get to have skin to skin contact right after birth, I did get to enjoy it when I went back to the room with Tyson. It is very important to get as much skin to skin contact as you can. Even though I was in a lot of pain, I was still able to have Tyson on my chest and be comfortable with him there. It was a great bonding experience that I could share with my newborn baby.

Myth: You will have a tough time breastfeeding if you had a c-section. People would tell me, "Your milk will come in a lot later and you might not be able to breastfeed at all because your body is confused. It does not realize it had a baby." *Oh trust me, it knows you had that baby, alright.* You will be in pain, and unable to move in the beginning, but if I could breastfeed, so too can you, Mama. It is very important for the baby to get the colostrum at the beginning that will help protect the baby from any infection. This might not be the case for everyone, but just know breastfeeding is a possibility even if you had a c-section, and of course, if it is **something you decide to do.** Whether you choose to breastfeed or formula feed, or do a mix of both; **fed is always best**.

The article also mentions, "Breastfeeding will not be impossible, but it will require a little patience. It's true, initiating breastfeeding takes a little longer for mothers who deliver via c-section than those who deliver vaginally. However, according to the American Congress of Obstetricians and Gynecologists (ACOG) the rates of breastfeeding are about the same between three and twenty-four months after delivery, no matter how you give birth. You may still be in pain after a c-section though, so try different ways of holding your baby. Dr. Schaffir suggests positioning your baby in a 'football hold' next to your breast instead of the 'cradle hold' on top of your stomach. If you're still struggling to breastfeed after a c-section, meet with a lactation consultant who can offer some tips to make the process a little easier." I went to a lactation consultant who taught me how to hold my baby. Do not be afraid to ask the nurses questions; they will be able to help you with breastfeeding and acquiring resources too. For me, I felt breastfeeding was one of the hardest tasks. Not because I had a c-section, but because it takes a lot of work. You are on a two to three hour feeding schedule and exhausted. Having major surgery does not help either. I was afraid to ask for help; I shouldn't have been and neither should you. Asking for help doesn't make you a failure. It makes you a better mama. Tyson did latch on, but I was not producing enough milk. Tyson's weight went down, and we had to supplement with formula. I felt as though I was letting him down because I had to give him formula. Why? Because I thought that breastfeeding was the best option for him. At the end of the day, *fed* is the best option. I did not want my baby to starve. I should never have felt ashamed of that. Neither should you, Mama! So I breastfed AND supplemented with formula. Best of both worlds.

Myth: If your first baby was born via c-section, it means that all your children will be birthed that way. No, this is not true. There is still a chance that if you decide to have another child, you could deliver vaginally. My midwife informed me it is possible for me to have a vaginal birth the second time around but I would have to wait two years. On parents.com it says, "Many doctors advise women to wait eighteen to twenty-four months after they've given birth before trying to conceive again, but this is especially true for those that have delivered by c-section. This timeout gives your body a chance to heal and recover from surgery. Research shows that getting pregnant less than six months after c-section can increase your risk of complications like a ruptured uterus or having a low birth weight baby during your next pregnancy. If you'd like to try for a vaginal birth next time (VBAC), you have even more reason to consider holding off conceiving, since studies have found that the rate of uterine rupture is higher during VBACs when it's been less than two years between deliveries." My mother in law delivered my husband, who was her firstborn, by c-section and her second child, vaginally. She did wait the two-year mark. It is possible; it just depends on the situation.

"If you do wish to deliver vaginally after a c-section, you will undergo what is known as a trial or labor after cesarean, or TOLAC. This trial will determine whether it's safe to move forward with the VBAC. Fortunately, the outcomes are positive for most women. According to ACOG, about sixty to eighty percent of women who undergo TOLAC deliver via vaginal birth successfully. Overall, a previous c-section will have little impact on future vaginal delivery."

I have always been a go-with-the-flow kind of person. Easy going, but I also need to have a plan, an idea of what will happen. However, when you are having a baby, things do not always go as planned. You may have a vision or even a foolproof plan of how you want things to go or what you think will happen. If it doesn't happen the way you planned, don't let yourself down. This is what happened to me. I felt let down because of the pressures that society places upon us. You are doing what is best for you and your family, and that is all that matters. It does not matter what anyone else says or thinks, it is your decision alone, and nobody else's. Don't doubt yourself. You are doing the right thing, Mama! You've got this! As long as you are happy, and your family is healthy and happy then, you did it! You are amazing - don't you ever forget that! You gave birth to a child. You created a human being. How amazing is that? So amazing. We as women are so hard on ourselves, don't be. Trust your motherly instincts; they are always right.

~ I would like to dedicate my chapter to my wonderful husband, Arynn, for always believing in me. To my son, Tyson, for inspiring me everyday and making me a MAMA. I love you both to the moon and back.

4

A DIFFERENT KIND OF BIRTH STORY

by Carrie Mazzei

"*Fear can be our greatest obstacle, and breath our greatest friend*"

Carrie Mazzei

Ask anybody who knows her and they will tell you that Carrie is most passionate about her work as a counsellor for children, youth and families; always approaching each new client with an open heart and mind, free of judgement or preconceived notions.

Carrie has always loved working with children, it's no surprise her favorite job is being a mom to her three amazing boys. When she is not working at her private practice, she can be found continuing her journey towards spiritual growth, self fulfillment, and happiness. For Carrie, happiness lies in spending quality time with her closest friends and family including the love of her life, her incredible husband of ten years. Carrie prides herself on being surrounded with genuine, loving souls and for a short time partnered up with three of those beautiful people to create a movement called One Small Change, inspiring people to create a better world for generations to come.

ig: @journey2freedom.services

"Your inner strength is invulnerable to fear."
~ Deepak Chopra

EAR, IT SEEMS TO BE EMBEDDED in every aspect of parenting. It starts in pregnancy and continues as our children grow. *Is my belly big enough? Am I eating the right foods? Is my baby getting enough milk? Am I damaging them by letting them cry it out? Is he too young to eat solids? What about allergies? Will he make friends at school? Will they be the right friends? Are they going to be safe on the road? Will he get into drugs?* and on and on and on. My first real experience with fear in parenthood came when I was pregnant with my first son. My doctors told me they found a soft marker for Down syndrome. I went home and cried my eyes out, and after about an hour, I surrendered to the realization that I was going to keep my baby regardless. I decided that I could not control the outcome and in that moment, knowing this was my first pregnancy and maybe my only (as no one knows what the future holds), I decided to just let go and enjoy every moment free from fear.

However, it didn't take long for fear to creep in again, all I had to do was switch on the t.v. or talk to other moms about the "horrifying" experience of childbirth. People describe the pain as excruciating. "The worst pain they've ever felt." My coworker told me that I will remember the pain for the rest of my life, but what scared me more than the pain they talked about was the thought of that huge needle going into my spine. To me, there was no greater fear than the epidural, but trust me when I tell you, I am no wonder woman. Pain is not something I seek out, and paper cuts can make me cry.

I knew I needed to find something and when I wasn't looking, that something found me. At the center where I was taking my prenatal class, I saw an advertisement for a hypnobirthing course. I signed up right away eager to find any solution to help me cope with this horrific pain everybody talks about. Hypnobirthing teaches you breathing and visualization techniques but more than that, it showed me we had rights. A right to question the doctor's advice, a right to ask questions about the things they were suggesting for you and your baby, and a right to create a birth plan that felt comfortable and right for you and your unborn child. We were also taught to trust in nature and our bodies. That our body would know what to do when the time came, and that millions of women before us had brought babies into this world, some in remote places on earth with very little support and often no medical intervention. I was ready; free from fear.

Unfortunately, not everyone shared the same enthusiasm for my birth plan. When my OB asked if she should set up an appointment with the anesthesiologist, I declined and let her know that I didn't want to have an epidural. She responded by tapping me on my shoulder and in a very patronizing tone said, "We'll see about that honey." That was all I needed to seal the deal; I would do this no matter what, because the second somebody tells me I can't do something, that's the moment I decide that nothing will stop me. She wasn't the only one though; I could hear the fear in my father's voice when he asked if I was *fucking nuts* for choosing not to have the epidural and making me promise to deliver in the hospital.

When I went into labor with my first son, I arrived at the hospital ready with a plan, and it didn't include fear, it was not welcome. The labor was long; thirty-six hours to be exact. I did a lot of walking and swaying, humming, and breathing. At one point the doctors recommended that I have my water broken to speed up the process. However, I held off for as long as I could, and when I felt ready, I allowed them to break my water. It didn't take long after that for the contractions to come on fast and furiously. I tried to remember how I handled the intense cravings when I quit smoking, never worrying about when the next craving would come, but just trying to be present in the moment and doing what I needed to do when the next craving hit. I applied that same concept to my labor. I did not concern myself with how much time had lapsed or how much time I had left to go. I focused on the present by taking it one contraction at a time. When thirty-six hours were over, and I held my son in my arms, I realized that I hadn't used hypnobirthing at all. I felt pain, a lot of it, especially towards the end when my body was telling me to push and my cervix was not quite there yet. I realized that it was sheer stubbornness and determination that had gotten me through.

Ten months later, I found out that I would have the chance to do it all over again. I was pregnant with my second, and determined to make some changes. For starters, I switched from a teaching hospital to a hospital which (I felt) would provide the kind of serene environment I needed to stay focused and calm during my labor. I also found a private instructor to brush up on the techniques I learned in my hypnobirthing class. This time, the focus was on the breathing exercises. I practiced that breathing exercise everywhere I could - when I was getting waxed, threaded and bleached, basically anytime I was volunteering to be tortured. I didn't know it then, but I was preparing for the impossible. A birth story I would have never believed had I not lived and experienced it, a birth story I have shared time and time again in the hopes of telling a new story about birth. A story where fear is replaced with complete and utter peace.

Brody was due on Dec 28th but was not too keen on coming out. I was almost a week past my due date and had to go in for ultrasounds almost daily. The doctors tried to convince me to induce labor even though he was a good size and there were no concerns. I remembered what I had learned in my hypnobirthing class, that I have a right to ask questions and refuse suggestions unless there is a risk to both myself and my unborn child. My intuition knew that my stubborn little sweetie would make his appearance when he was ready, not when everyone else was. Additionally, I also knew being induced would bring on my contractions fast and furiously, making it more difficult to get in the "zone," so I waited and I walked… A LOT. I walked around the entire mall two times, went home and lost my mucus plug. He was ready.

I went into labor on Jan 3rd, in the evening. When we first checked into the hospital, I tried walking as I had done with my first labor. It didn't feel quite right, so I tried soaking in a bath for a bit and that too was not getting me into the mindset I was looking for. Finally, I decided to lay on the bed partially on my side with a pillow supporting my belly. I closed my eyes and began my breathing exercise. I used the breath technique I had learned during my hypnobirthing class; breathe in *one… two… three… four,* and out *five… six… seven… eight,* repeating. "Relax, relax, relax," with each out breath. I focused all of my breath into my contraction. I didn't speak, I just breathed for hours, I got myself to a place where I could feel the contractions and NO PAIN, I repeat NO PAIN associated with it. My husband, mom, and sisters who were all in the room thought I was sleeping. Since I chose to switch hospitals, there weren't a hundred doctors coming in all the time probing and grabbing at me. It was just one nurse, one amazing nurse who stayed with me for almost twelve hours, only checking a few times to see how dilated I was. When it was time to push, I remember the nurse telling me to brace myself for the ring of fire (The burning or stinging sensation you feel when your baby's head crowns). But amazingly, I was so relaxed, I never did feel the ring of fire, or any pain at all; just a sense of calm. It was the kind of birth I had always dreamed of but never really believed could happen. At the end of it all, my mother turned to the doctor that had delivered my baby and asked if more women were choosing to give birth naturally, and his response was, "No, most people don't like pain." I wanted to tell him *where to go and how to get there* but realized that he too, probably didn't believe in the possibility of birth without pain. I learned many things from my birthing experience, things I have always wanted to share with others.

1. We have a voice, we can ask questions and have control over our bodies and our births.
2. A pain-free delivery IS possible.
3. Our breath is our greatest ally in creating a space of calm in our bodies.
4. This is about us, about what we feel is right for ourselves and for our unborn children. Surrendering to wherever this journey takes us.

I remember my hypnobirthing teacher telling us about her second birth. She tried for hours to use hypnobirthing but said that the pain was so intense she ended up asking for the epidural. I loved her for sharing that with us. It gave me permission to surrender to whatever was going to come my way.

As parents, we forever question our choices; wondering if we are saying the right thing, and doing the right thing. Too much of this, too little of that. We fear the decisions we've made and are held prisoner by our fear of the future. Don't worry, Mama; we've got this. You've got this. Just like birth, sometimes things in life don't always go as planned. We don't know what the future holds, but what we do have is right now, and if we can stay here right now, in the present anchored only by our breath, fear can never take hold. We will always be free.

~ I dedicate this chapter to my three little bears Tano, Brody, and Riley, I didn't know my heart had the capacity to love so much until the Divine sent you to me. To my loving husband, you are my rock; my everything. And to my forever inspiration, my own beautiful mother. Last but not least I dedicate this to all the incredible mothers out there, trying their very best, I see you, I think you're amazing, you've got this, Mama.

5

THERE IS HONEY
IN HEARTACHE

by Kristin Hallett

"Sometimes, closure arrives years later. Long after you stopped searching for it."

Kristin Hallett

This is Kristin Hallett's second - in-print - writing venture. She is also the author of the children's book, *Bee Love*. In addition, Kristin's personal writing and musings can be found on her Instagram account, @Word. Honey. She lives in Calgary, Alberta, Canada and works for the Calgary Flames - on the media relations side - connecting the team with the community. Kristin is the mother of her baby girl, Perrin, and the luckiest wife to Justin. When Kristin is not writing or getting in trouble for cheering in the press box (at Flames games), she can be found on top of, and/or climbing the Rockies, in her backyard. If not there, she is drinking overpriced coffee, saving wine from bottles and connecting with her diverse batch of soul friends and family.

www.beelovebook.com
ig: @KristinHallett | @word.honey
t: @Kristin_Hallett

"It's time for me to exhale you.
It's time for you to leave me.
Not because I don't love you...
But, because your journey is not mine and mine is not yours.
Perhaps, we will meet again, on the other side of this mountain.
I'll keep climbing, My Love."
~ word.honey

I SIGNED UP TO write THIS CHAPTER the way I do most things: impulsively. I'm *that* mom. The mom who commits to something and, directly afterwards, starts plotting about how she can get out of it without sounding 1) Lazy, and 2) Like a quitter. Ugh. I have a four-month-old, surely, she's the ticket. My perfect out! The truth is when I sat down to write my story... it felt so, well... common. What I planned to write about, in hindsight, isn't groundbreaking at all. It's exactly (statistically speaking) what nearly ALL of us experience at some point in our life.

I had a miscarriage. *So, what? So did my aunt, my friend, my friend's friend, and my sister... twice!* Then it hit me, what if that's why I need to keep writing? Because, it is something "so common" and yet, so uncommonly talked about. Because, in losing my baby, I discovered an underground sisterhood of women, who all hung in the shadows, and quietly weathered the storm of the most misunderstood grief. The kind of storm many weather alone - as it makes people uncomfortable. Or, when it is finally talked about, it's from calm waters or the shore. After the storm has passed.

However, in the eye of it, I was absolutely swallowed.

I've learned a lot about two things: grief, and what an empty hole in my stomach, literally and figuratively, feels like.

Let's begin with grief:

"Some people are not meant to grow with... they are meant to grow from." ~ word.honey

I wrote that right after I lost Will. I wrote a lot after I had to say goodbye to him. Made an alias and everything. I lost a baby boy nearly halfway through my pregnancy. When I think about how consumed I became, how the entire experience rocked my core and reframed my brain, it almost seems like another lifetime now. And believe me, I know how "common" losing a baby is. I have been told over and over by those, who I know are well-intentioned, who haven't experienced it. So, on the one hand, I look back and think to myself, *Girl, you were batshit crazy,* and I even smirk a little and sit light-hearted with myself - the same way I sit and shake my head about how I acted with past boyfriends or eyebrow plucking choices. Who was *that* girl?

Oh, but on certain days, at certain times, the heaviness consumes me, and I cry. Even now, with a sweet, little baby girl, who wouldn't be here otherwise. This, more often than not, happens during a quiet moment, when a rainbow splashes somewhere in my house. And, I know there are a handful of scientific explanations as to why the light hits the walls that way. Documented evidence as to how and why colors dance across the floor and rest inside my palm that way. But... some days, I let science walk. It takes a backseat to the energy I feel all around me. Some days, I just stare into that light and say, "Hello, Will. I miss you." And, yes, I still cry.

Do you?

Because I think I know why I do.

I don't think it's just because I lost a baby. I am beginning to realize that what I also cry about is the part of myself that I lost, too. *That* girl, she was just a little bit more fun. And, I loved her. She was just a little bit more innocent. I miss her, too.

♥ ♥ ♥

We were there, with the ultrasound tech; my husband and I. We held hands and made small talk about her work.

"How long have you done this?" I asked. She was quite new. I went on to assume, out loud, "It must be so hard to see a happy couple and know something is wrong before they do?"

She replied, "Yes," and then, all of a sudden, stood up.

"I can't seem to get a clear image," she murmured, without eye contact. "Maybe you could stand up and move a little, and the baby will shift for us to take another look."

She exited the room as I followed her suggestion and hopped off the examination table. My shirt was still tucked into my bra, and my belly was exposed with goopy glisten. There was a sheet of medical tissue paper hanging from my pants to protect my jeans from getting gooped. Now standing, it looked like a hilarious, heavily starched skirt. I began doing some sort of hula-esque dance as my husband cracked up laughing. It was one of those awkward dances where you pretend to be seductive, "You know you want it," but is NOT sexy at all, and only for the deep belly laughs. I danced, all the while thinking of the baby, in my belly, doing somersaults and loving every minute of it. No doubt thrilled for the wild ride of a family he was about to join.

That was her. The "me" I loved. She died that day. You see, the "quite new," ultrasound tech never came back. Instead, the lead tech, alongside the doctor, entered the room.

> *"You think you are sad, but you are sadly mistaken*
> *Numb people are sad.*
> *You? You are quite the opposite.*
> *And, it hurts. It hurts because it was real and loving too much is*
> *all you know."* ~ word.honey

I was scheduled to "say goodbye" to Will one week following that ultrasound. Here's the kicker, the week we spent, leading up to the procedure, he was very much alive and growing. I couldn't shake the sound of his perfect heartbeat.

But, that's all I'm going to say about that. I could go on... drown in the sad details. To be honest, the mess that was inside of my stomach is not relevant, right now. You see, I am diverging here because I have observed what starts happening. The twisted pain that is comparison seeps in.

"Oh, I knew someone who was full term."

"Well, at least you can get pregnant."

"That happened to me, except I was single and alone."

And, well, it just doesn't matter. So, what have I learned about grief? Grief is grief. It is often misunderstood, and that's okay. It is yours, and yours alone. You don't need to explain it. If you want to cry, out of the blue, two years after a miscarriage, cry. Grief does not belong on a scale nor can it be measured. Moreover, with grief, there is no healthy place for comparison. Comparison comes along, disguised as pain, or a front for discomfort. Grief cannot and should not be compared. It should be held and nurtured the same way you had dreamed of holding and nurturing that tiny human who once was. That dream that was cut short.

♥ ♥ ♥

So, what happens now with that gaping hole left inside your stomach? Well...

"Sometimes, closure arrives years later. Long after you stopped searching for it. You're just sitting there laughing this laugh that is unapologetically yours. As it trails off, the corners of your mouth hug your face, and it hits you, 'I'm happy.' It's just like that. With no fanfare or epiphany. Suddenly, you are grateful for goodbyes that carried you to this moment; to the space you are now holding."
~ word.honey

That's what happens. You change and adjust your sails. You learn to move with the ebbs and flows, reveling in the calm waters and sunny skies somedays, while still honoring the once turbulent memory of a storm that swallowed you whole. You may not be the person you were, and it's okay to miss her still. But, the person you are becoming, all of a sudden, appears pretty badass. She has layers and strength.

The emptiness that Will left behind, inside of me, I channeled into a children's book, *Bee Love*. Rather, *In a World Where You Can Be Anything... Bee Love*. The story came to me in a dream, when I was three months pregnant with him. I never nap. Ever. However, on this particular day, I walked past our soon-to-be nursery and drifted inside. I sprawled out on the guest mattress, which still occupied the space, (despite asking my husband to move it to the basement, multiple times... insert raging hormones, here). There, looking a lot like I was in the beginning stages of crafting a snow angel, I soaked up all the stillness that our baby's room held. I consciously inhaled the quiet, calm, knowing full well there would be 3am screams and feedings, in this very space, very soon. Right then and there, I fell asleep. I, Kristin Hallett, had a nap. And during that nap, I had the most vivid dream about a magical, little honey bee. Now, don't get me mixed up with someone all sweet and innocent, here. This dream was extremely atypical, for me. My dreams are usually erotic, dark, or a combination of both! This dream played out like a vivid, colorful poem. I had an urge to write the dream down, instantaneously. So, I did. I typed it into my phone and never thought about it again. It wasn't until he was gone, a few months later, and I found the story in my notes, that I crumbled. Ugly cried. Could not come to grips with reading it aloud. I knew, right then and there, his "soul" purpose was this story. This message. For someone who never planned to write a children's book, I felt driven in a different way to see it through. I think I felt delivering this book would replace the loss of delivering that child. And, well, it did. I self-published *Bee Love*, and hosted a book launch, almost a year to the day Will returned up to the stars.

I, naturally, am deeply connected to the book, but never considered or anticipated other people (especially mothers) would be too. The local printer I worked with in Calgary, firmly advised me to start small and only print one hundred copies. In their opinion, that may even be too many. They had seen these little "passion projects," before, and how time and time again, the books gathered dust. NO. I would print five hundred. Even if they sat in my basement for ten years, I set a goal to pay this story forward to five hundred people. And... guess what? I did. Well, Will did. *Bee Love* sold out in one week. One week.

The book, of course, belongs to Will. But, on the very last page, it acknowledges all of us with:

> *"The* Will *to love, the* Will *to smile, despite what the world throws your way... And, the* Will *to get back up and try again."*

It is then dedicated to:

"Every little soul whose wings were ready long before their parents' hearts would ever be."

Every time *Bee Love* got into the hands of parents who had experienced loss, that empty hole in my stomach would fill up a bit... and a little bit more. Soon, retailers were contacting me to carry it, and my husband and I were charging $20,000 on our credit card to print an additional fifteen hundred copies. It's currently in the hands of a major publisher... *Bee Love* keeps spreading.

So, now comes the part where I wish I could end this chapter. Hit it out of the park with a closing remark about how my experience of loss gave me unwavering strength. Well, I can tell you it did, in many ways – but, not entirely.

Because, I got pregnant, again, and I wasn't excited. Instead, I was terrified. I now knew that anything was possible and I wasn't "Invincible-Pregnant-Kristin," anymore. I was "Prepare-Yourself-Pregnant-Kristin." All the apps that tell you your baby is the size of a mango or mongoose (or whatever!) made me feel sad. Well, sad and mad. I'd already reached those milestones. It was as if my body was seizing up from anxiety. Why? Because I didn't trust it; it broke my last baby. *My body does unimaginable things to babies.* Who thinks that? Let alone says it? I did. Once I was far enough along in my pregnancy that our baby could sustain life outside my tummy, I wanted it out of me. I wanted it out before something bad happened. My ob-gyn, who is the oh-BGY-nicest assured me this was – of course (that word again!), COMMON! My blood pressure began to rise, which I know was my mental doing, and we agreed that being induced, two weeks early, was the right decision. And there she was. SHE. My five pound, Perrin Sapphia. Even when she was born, I was subconsciously prepared, just in case, that something bad might happen. Could happen. Prepared to hear something was wrong. *And, she? Where was my boy?* I had gotten caught up in a fantasy about having a son. Poor Perrin. No one can compete with a fantasy, as it's not real and she was. Is. Every day, over and over, this mantra manifested itself in my head: "She is here, and she is healthy." I would repeat it like a skipping record, "She is here, and she is healthy."

Perrin was two weeks old the first night we were alone together, as my husband was away at a work function. In a quiet and alert moment of hers, I looked at her and said, "I'm sorry." And then I cried. I cried harder than I have ever cried before. She watched me, mesmerized with her eyes that would soon turn brown, like mine. I know now that the tears were me shedding all the pent-up anxiety. The tears were the already thick and heavy mom guilt I possessed for not growing her in nothing less than a loving environment. Tears, also, for not being instantaneously grateful for a little girl, as a feminist mother should be. I cried and cried and, in those last drops of tears, released the life I had envisioned with Will. I exhaled and made space for Perrin. That was the night my little girl entered through the broken opening in my heart to live forever.

I would like to end this chapter by circling back to how I began it by minimizing my feelings and expressing how very common losing a baby is. I did this because I know full-well someone, out there, has suffered far worse. Their not-so-common heartache deserves the stage. Deserves this platform. Who am I to cry this river? Except, would you like to know what else is common? Divorce. Cancer. LOVE. And they all rip us open and make us fall to our knees. But most of all, our commonalities are also a universal language. It is what connects us inextricably with each other. Please feel free to heal and never question the validity of your pain. It is not there to compare; it is there to connect. *In a world where you can be anything, Bee Love.*

~ I would like to thank my husband, Justin, for always being blind to gender roles and never letting me sell myself short or say no to an opportunity. I would also like to thank the sisterhood of strong women in my life, who held my heart through "my storm," free of judgement and expectation. Finally to Will, for his lessons-in-love and to sweet Perrin, for showing me what joy truly feels like.

Section 2

DISCOVERING JOY IN CHAOS AND COPING WITH CHANGE

FEATURING
Habiba Jessica Zaman
Valerie Steele
Melissa Smith
Sherri Marie Gaudet
Jessica Janzen Olstad

OPENING COMMENTARY BY
Sabrina Greer

YOU DID IT. It can seem unbelievable, but you've made it through. Pat yourself on the back and pour yourself a glass of champagne because you have created life like the incredible, magical goddess you are. A human being lived inside your body for the better part of a year, and somehow (however traumatic or graceful your delivery) has now entered this vast, unfamiliar world. Congratulations to you! What an unthinkable feat. Now for the inevitable question: *WHAT'S NEXT, what the heck do we do now?* That's right; you are not alone. We all have some version of these thoughts; of this question.

Not only are you expected to protect this tiny person, but this child is one hundred percent dependent on you for everything. Food (which, in many cases, you must make with your body), shelter, safety, sleep, bodily functions, I mean EVERYTHING. It becomes very challenging to take care of yourself, to think about anybody besides the baby. I mean, it's even challenging to know what day it is or to go to the bathroom. This is why this stage is referred to as **the fourth trimester**, that babe is attached, and still very much an extension of you.

You want a shower, too bad. You want to sleep in, ha, sorry Mama, not for a while. You've got other kids that want attention, call in your new babysitter, *Dora The Explorer.* This tiny tyrant takes over every aspect of your life. Oh, and you must do all of this while your body is healing from an internal wound the circumference of a watermelon and the trauma of forty weeks living with a parasite (an organism that lives in or on another body (its host) and benefits by deriving nutrients - literally, I'm not trying to be cheeky.) I do not tell you this to frighten or overwhelm you. I say this to commend you for being a superhero, warrior, and to provide you comfort in knowing that you are not alone. You've totally got this. Let me explain and share the most valuable piece of advice that was ever given to me.

It's all temporary! Let me repeat: IT'S ALL TEMPORARY.

You see, this section too had a common theme, another union bringing us together in all our new-mom glory. Regardless of how different our pregnancies, labors, and deliveries were, we, at some point, were all terrified, clueless, and majorly freaking out, at least on some level. This is entirely normal; you are totally normal! You will inevitably experience infinite changes in your personal bubble, regardless of how prepared you think you are or how anxiously you awaited this arrival. The body you once knew, will be temporarily unrecognizable. Normal. Emotionally, you will feel different, very different. Also, normal. You will be all-consumed with incredible love, uncontrollable hormones, and a side of sleep deprivation. You will feel emotions stronger than ever before, magnified and amplified beyond comprehension by an invisible force. **All normal**.

Please do us a favor, do yourself a favor, and be gentle and kind to yourself, with your journey. Do not put unrealistic expectations on this process. Remember what you have just accomplished, what your body has just pulled off. You produced a human being, a real person. Look in the mirror and instead of seeing loose skin and stretch marks, see battle scars and be proud. Instead of giving in to the feelings of resentment and sadness, know that your body just disposed of all of its mood elevating hormones with this beautiful child and you're literally not in control of your emotions right now, so just let go, breathe. Don't compare your journey. Everyone is different, and all things take time. Motherhood is not a race, or a competitive sport, it is a slow hike through rough terrain. Remove self-expectations and never allow anyone else's opinions to penetrate your armor. Take this precious time to bond with your little bundle and stop paying attention to everyone and everything else.

I have done many things in my life such as jumping out of airplanes, diving meters below the ocean's surface in a cage to pat the snouts of great white sharks and traveled most of the world. I have fallen in love, and had multiple broken hearts. I've feared for my life while being held at gunpoint, and seen indescribable beauty. Through all of this, I can still state, without hesitation, that there is no comparable emotion or existing adjective that can describe holding your baby for the first time. Whether he is handed over to you by your doctor after surgery, or she arrives blissfully, naturally, and according to plan in your bathtub. Whether you're holding hands through an incubator in the NICU or you deliver on the side of a highway, NOTHING beats that first contact.

The first time those little eyes open, the first sounds that exit their tiny mouths. Knowing that what was merely a foreign object inhabiting your body for forty weeks, is now a person. It is quite incredible what a woman's body is capable of. All this awe, this miracle of human life, is a wonderful distraction for all of this extra baggage you're now lugging around, so try to be in the moments you are in and embrace your beautiful madness.

He will eventually sleep through the night, which means you will sleep again. She will gain weight soon, so you need not worry. He will stop crying before your ears explode, and she will grow out of that phase, whatever it may be. You will get to bathe again, I pinky promise and yes, your vagina will heal even if it has some new charm. I want to encourage you to view all things in the now, in the right now, knowing that the discomfort will pass soon. I hope the stories in this section inspire you to find joy in every morsel of this journey. Ask for help when you need it, find support, consult your village and take care of yourself first. It may sometimes seem like you are at the bottom of a dark hole with no way out, but there is light. It may look like you are in a never-ending cycle of bodily fluids and dirty laundry, but *this too shall pass*. There is so much joy and beauty within this chaos, you must choose to see it and embrace it for what it is. You've got this, Mama!

6

DEVELOPING
FROM THE NEGATIVES

by Habiba Jessica Zaman

"Each stage of motherhood is another transformation of the wonderment that is you."

Habiba Jessica Zaman

Habiba Jessica Zaman, NCC LPC has a master's degree in professional counseling specializing in trauma and is the therapist and owner of North Star of Georgia Counseling. With fifteen years of work experience in the counseling field including counseling, advocacy, guidance, and education, she believes that as awareness of one's fears, perception, desires, and strengths increase, one can make successful life changes. Self-awareness, by becoming more honest with oneself, can initiate the authenticity that often results in healing, transformation, and living a fuller life. She has nine publications that started with a children's book published in 2012, *But I'm Just Playing,* and her latest, *Beautifully Bare, Undeniably You* due to be released in 2018. Habiba is of Bangladeshi and American descent. She has two children and lives in Atlanta, Georgia with her family.

fb: northstarofgeorgia | habibajessicazaman

"For beautiful eyes, look for the good in others; for beautiful lips,
speak only words of kindness; and for poise, walk with
the knowledge that you are never alone."
~ Audrey Hepburn

*T*HE DAY HAS FINALLY COME, *the beginning of my greatest adventure yet. Here he is, my most priceless treasure, nestled and sleeping in the crook of my arm. I am happy, I am joyous, and overwhelmed... no, I meant to say I am overflowing with love. Yes, honestly, this is the best thing that has happened to me, and I know it. I am thankful, and I am numb... Haha, I'm sorry, again, I meant to say I am fulfilled. This moment is what I have been dreaming of, he is finally here, and we are finally home. I am crying, again. It's just the blues as the doctors said. I am okay. I have to be okay. Only sometimes, I don't feel that okay, but if I say that out loud... what will that mean? That I am ungrateful? That I am weak? I got this... no really... I got this... just sometimes, it feels like this got me.*

Anyone who has experienced or witnessed motherhood will laughingly share that the first few weeks are filled with emotional upheaval. Imagine trying to adjust to the changes in your body (*What IS up with this deflated balloon of a belly*), the hormonal changes (*More goop? Am I shedding?*), the sleep deprivation (*Huh? Who? Was I just drooling?*), always second guessing how to hold, feed, burp, change, or put the baby to sleep, AND taking care of yourself, your relationship, and the house. Who wouldn't feel overwhelmed? It becomes tricky, however, to distinguish the difference between the baby blues and postpartum depression (PPD) because they have symptoms in common. Is it the usual and expected stress and exhaustion of new parenthood or is it something more? While the baby blues ease with time, postpartum depression can be intense and persists for a longer duration of time.

According to the American Psychiatric Association, about ten percent of new mothers develop PPD, but some experts believe the number is even higher because many women don't seek treatment or even speak up about it. The stigma associated with postpartum depression and other mental health issues are still prevalent, and many women will stay silent and suffer in secrecy to avoid judgment. First and foremost, it is imperative for new mothers to know that you are not alone. 40-80% of new mothers report the baby blues. Be kind to yourself, and leave the messages of self-loathing at the hospital. I am here to assure you, that you are enough.

So, how do we know the difference? Baby blues are an emotional state of unhappiness, self-doubt, nervousness, and exhaustion that begin a few days after delivery and go away on their own within a week or two. However, if your feelings seem unusually intense and last longer than two weeks straight, it may be worth considering whether you have a more serious condition or postpartum depression.

There's just so much to do. I am at home all alone, and my husband is at work. I loved being alone - I'm an introvert! But I've never felt so alone in my life. He is so perfect, and his smile is just everything to me. Mama's little shami name. Then there is the projectile vomit, I mean, how can that much milk come out of this little body?! I'm so sorry, baby, mama is so sorry. He is crying, and I am crying, I am so sorry baby. You deserve so much more than what I can give to you, why AM I SURPRISED? I should have known better. I can't do this. I mean I can; I know how to. I have a master's degree in human development for crying out loud! I was meant to be a mother; this is not how it is supposed to feel. I feel so alone. When he sleeps, I should be sleeping, but it's just better not to. There's too much to do around the house - or that's what I tell myself. It's better when I am busy to ignore these thoughts sometimes. It is so hard to just settle down, and quiet my mind. I feel trapped in this house. This is why I can't sleep... things just need to get done though. There is so much to do and not enough time or help to do it. I am crying again. Really? NOTHING IS WRONG!

The surest way to gauge if you have postpartum depression is to notice the intensity of the emotions you feel. Overwhelmed could feel more like irritation and anger coupled with lack of patience and feeling out of control. It could also be hopelessness and helplessness to where you feel weak or like a complete failure. On the other hand, you could feel completely numb and a sense of emptiness and sadness to the depths of your soul. Tearfulness could be more like endless crying even when there is no actual reason to be crying. You could feel like you are wandering in a fog with no sight of this coming to an end, and feel apart from everyone around you. It could feel so intense that you may have thoughts of finding some way to end this misery or justifying that your baby would be better off without you.

Maybe you're doing everything right. You exercise, eat healthy, and also take your vitamins. You have a healthy spirituality and also practice yoga. You're thinking, *Why can't I just get over this?* You feel as though you should be able to snap out of it, but you can't. This was my greatest struggle. I kept thinking, *I have a master's degree in mental health with a focus on human development and trauma. I, of all people, should not feel this way. I should be able to manage my emotions; I should be able to cope. I should know where this is coming from. So what does it say about me as a professional? That I am entrapped in the chains of my mind?* I'll tell you what someone should have told me - NOT A DAMNED THING!

There are things you can do to minimize the intensity of postpartum depression. You are already one step ahead because you are reading this book! Reading is something that has always helped me be aware, identify, and categorize what I am experiencing. Since you now know what the symptoms look like and how to recognize the difference, you will be able to feel more in control of the chaos that is within you as well. You know you are not alone in this, and you are not losing your mind. Read up on what to expect both during and after the delivery; especially, the books that take a more realistic approach rather than the romanticized version of what to expect. Being a mother and the journey of becoming a mother is one of nature's marvels, and it can also be one of the most challenging experiences we face as women.

Communication is essential in all successful relationships. Be it with family, friends, romantic partners, or colleagues. It helps us to arrive at shared understandings and resolve differences. It is most crucial to communicate with your partner and support systems about your needs the first months of parenthood as they are the most emotionally tender and physically exhausting months. In theory, it should be a simple, almost intuitive, process.

Unfortunately, due to differences in interpretation, listening style, delivery style, and non-shared meanings, much of what we say, or mean to say, gets lost in translation, despite our best intentions. We say one thing and the other person hears something else or we intended one thing and something completely different was inferred. Add in the difficulties inherent with communications over different mediums such as email and text and the misunderstandings can quickly escalate. These are all potential sources of conflict in communication.

It is attractive to blame our communication partner when things go awry. Because outside our professional endeavors, we often communicate from a place of emotion instead of approaching it strategically. Hence, it may be difficult to identify your responsibility in communicating effectively. When we communicate with loved ones or close friends, we feel as though they should "just get it" and when they don't, we assign blame (i.e., they never listen) and often, frustration, and resentment ensue. Similar to the languages of love[1] and apology, communication requires us to think about our communication partner's style and avoid unintentionally causing them to feel attacked or defensive. In short, we help foster open communication by using various skills and strategies.

First, and possibly most importantly, we do not have the right to define the other person's existence or how they perceive things for them. Stop and take a moment to let that sink in. Just how you are entitled to your position, your worldview, your way of being, so are they. Although many of us are taught to believe in the existence of objective truths and right versus wrong, no one stance or perception is better than the other. Until one can accept this notion to be true, they will be incapable of having genuine or effective communication. Because, when you hold the belief that you are right and they are wrong, then during a friendly debate or in the aftermath of a heated argument, you will have

....

1 Chapman, G. (2015). *The 5 Love Languages: The Secret to Love That Lasts*. Northfield Publishing. Chicago.

your guard up which will emanate through your posture, tone, and even the efficacy of your listening skills.

You will be unable to see the other person's point of view as valid, and empathy will be inauthentic. In these instances, you are likely to spend most of your energy drumming up your fabulous ret and sharpening our powers of persuasion, instead of hearing what is being said. So, what do you do? **Listen.** Listen as though you really want to know what this person is thinking and try to follow their thought patterns. Try to understand their worldview. Listen for how they came to this realization and what factors from their past experiences helped shape their ideas and values. Give them the respect and space to articulate their rationale and allow them to feel accepted as they are. Remember, intelligence is having the ability to understand and entertain a point of view without feeling obligated to accept it.

The second essential principle of communication is that for a person to understand where you are coming from, it is necessary to share it in a way that reaches past their conscious defenses. This may not be as crucial in casual conversations but is imperative in meaningful communication. Typically, in these instances of awkward conversations, we begin discussions by taking a defensive posture and justifying our stance. We start out already prepared to defend ourselves and our reasoning on why we have the right to say, feel, or think a certain way. We do this in our misguided attempt to justify our existence failing to remember that we already have the right to be there and be, say, and do exactly what we want!

So, I will share with you a process I have found to be effective in getting your communication partner to truly understand your perspective and "step into your shoes" for a moment. It is a five-step process initially developed by Gottman listed below:

1. State your feelings
2. Give the reasons that explain WHY you had each one of those feelings
3. List the triggers
4. Assume responsibility for the role you played in the situation
5. Identify solutions for the future

One of the most essential tools for building a healthy relationship is knowing how to process and present your position in a way that helps both partners learn from it and arrive at some resolution.

Months had passed since we started fighting. It seemed like every conversation that lasted more than a couple of minutes quickly turned to shame and blame in one form or another. I was guilty of it too, although rationalized my behavior which ranged from passive aggressive to just plain aggressive. He provoked me. He infuriates me. He is mean to me. One night, as the tears flowed, I decided I wanted a different narrative. This person was a part of my life and would continue in this capacity until our dying breath. We were linked. I had to do better; we had to do better.

I took out a piece of plain unlined paper and started writing... Step one.

You make me feel like you don't trust me or respect me (feeling). When you ask me questions and then hyper-focus on one thing I said or refuse to accept my answer or explanation (because), I feel invalidated and voiceless, like what I have to say doesn't matter (trigger). I know that sometimes I try to communicate essential topics when I am overly upset and because of that, it may be difficult for you to see that what you perceive as defensiveness is just me being passionate (responsibility). As we move through this life, I will try to take a break before I approach important topics so that I can do so without getting so upset (solution).

The list continued. Paragraph after paragraph. Complete with bullet points and sub-points, I carefully outlined how our attempts at communication had failed. It was easier than I thought, but then again, I love making lists.

Being able to invoke this communication style is beneficial in conflict resolution. It is often difficult for people to experience genuine empathy in high emotion and high conflict situations, especially in those cases where you feel compelled to protect and promote your position. Empathy is not always instinctual for everyone and may also be situational (e.g., I can empathize with the following conditions). Being able to see the validity of a different point or worldview, even without accepting it or adopting it, can help move communication forward instead of bringing it to a screeching halt.

Another helpful strategy is to make time and do the things that bring YOU joy. At first, telling yourself that each day needs to have an element of joy in it can be useful. These injections of joy are essential to transforming our thinking because, without it, we are frequently unable to change the circumstances we encounter. By focusing on attaining interludes of joy throughout our days, we have the power to change our outlook and regain a sense of control, even within stressful situations.

You can ease into it gently by thinking of five things that bring you joy. Write them down so they are tangible and you can return to the list when you are in need of a boost or when you forget that you have strategies in place to achieve joy. Once you've identified those five things, the next step is to determine ways to incorporate them into your routine for a minimum of ten minutes a day, because remember, we want these boosts of joy to be consistent. Although tempting, for this practice to be truly successful and sustainable, it is crucial that these things have nothing to do with spending money and are not dependent on other people. Relying on material objects or other consumer goods purchased with money can quickly lead to debt or despair when we are not able to attain the object of our desire - potentially eliciting the opposite effect of joy. Avoiding reliance on other people is somewhat more nuanced. Many times, we seek solace in the presence, affection, or attention of friends, family, and loved ones. For me, my children are my greatest source of joy. Before them, I honestly never thought I was capable of feeling joy and even when I experience it now, I forget all my woes for a moment. But having your joy be contingent on someone or something else has a fatal flaw - that someone or something can (and will) let you down, even if it is unintentional.

For example, let's say I had a trying day at the office and I am on my way to pick up my children, full of desire and expectation to have a beautiful afternoon with them to erase all that's gone wrong with my day. As soon as we walk through the front door, before even having the chance to take off my shoes, the boys start fighting over a toy, and the youngest is having a tantrum that would put the Tasmanian devil to shame... What happens to my joy then?

If we put our happiness in the hands of another to hold, they will drop it every time, and our attempt at happiness will be shattered, or at the very least, compromised. Please do not misunderstand my stance on the importance of friends and family. The people in our lives will, of course, be sources of influence for our experiences of happiness, joy, and excitement. However, they should not be the ones in charge of it - that job must reside solely with you.

One final morsel of guidance: **Remember who you are, and when in doubt, always bring to the forefront of your mind and heart, who you were before you became a mother.** I am Ryu and Luca's mom, yes... But, I am also a lot more along with that. Be explicit in identifying the growth and change and avoid the common trap of taking these things for granted. Celebrate what makes you so uniquely you and recognize that this new label of being a mom is an extension of who you already were. Allow yourself the grace to grow and evolve into who you want to be, and embrace the journey of who you will become. Each stage of motherhood is another transformation of the wonderment that is **you**.

~ To Shalon Irving. She was tenacious and unrelenting in this endeavor because she believed in this message and she believed in me. She was determined to bring to others the understanding, peace, and self-love she worked so hard to achieve. I could not have done this without her.

7

OUR GA1 WARRIOR

by Valerie Steele

"To show our children they too can be unstoppable is the ultimate gift."

Valerie Steele

Valerie Steele has an adventurous and determined spirit. She has spent the majority of her life seeking the unfamiliar. Whether through gorilla trekking in Rwanda, white water rafting along the Nile, hiking Cinque Terre's coastal trails, practicing yoga in Nepal, or biking through Tuscany, these experiences have all illuminated her heart with gratitude. She enjoys the beauty of nature and journaling. She is a teacher by trade and a writer by heart. Valerie's late grandmother instilled the love of books and reading in her as a child. She has had a number of her articles published in local newspapers. Valerie is a graduate of the University of Guelph and the University of Ottawa. She is passionate about empowering girls and women. Valerie truly believes you can do anything that you set your mind to, which she mastered from her amazing parents. Their positive and selfless support is unwavering and she is forever thankful. Valerie believes that adversity can also bring opportunity. Valerie has taught middle school students for fourteen years. Before becoming an intermediate level teacher, she taught horseback riding lessons for many years to adults and children with special needs. She has also taught at a teacher's college in China, traveled to India, Nepal, Kenya, Uganda, Denmark, and various other countries. Valerie now lives in Heartlake, Ontario, Canada with her husband and daughter, with the dream of showing her daughter the beauty of the world.

val@birjareno.ca
ig: @steelebirja
fb: @valeriesteele
t: @valerie849

"You gain strength, courage and confidence by every experience
in which you really stop to look fear in the face.
You must do the thing which you think you cannot do."
~ Eleanor Roosevelt

The Beginning

The sun rays beamed through my car windows as I drove along the country roads, it was surreal to think that I was finally driving to my baby shower. Attending more showers than I could count, a feeling of warm gratitude came over me. As I looked down at my mighty belly, I imagined who this little person might become and what it would be like, once I became a mother. In that moment, I pictured everything from mom and baby yoga classes, library programs, to swimming classes, and little did I know that the Universe had other plans for us. Our parenting preparation checklist and prenatal classes could not have prepared us on how to become parents of a child with a rare metabolic condition. The reality I experienced as a new mother was very different than the one I had envisioned.

In a society that always pushes us to consume more protein, we have spent the entirety of our daughter's life avoiding it. I had a healthy pregnancy without any complications. Our incredible daughter was born on August 19th, 2016 at 5:59pm. Overwhelmed with emotion and exhaustion, we could not believe that we were holding our perfect baby girl. She passed all the routine tests and examinations with flying colors.

For six days, we thought we had a typical healthy baby. For six days, we had the usual concerns of new parents. *Is our baby latching and feeding enough? Is our baby too cold or too hot?* We watched our precious baby girl's chest rise and fall every time she slept and felt relief with every sound. We examined every little facial feature and knew she was our beautiful miracle. It was the most fierce, and protective love I have ever experienced.

Then on day six, that phone call came from our doctor. It changed our lives forever. All I remember hearing on the other end was our doctor say, "Your daughter has been diagnosed with a rare genetic disease that could affect her brain." I immediately started crying and she said not to do so, or my milk supply would stop. She then told me she had already contacted my husband and that he was on his way home from work to pick us up. We were instructed to take our daughter to the emergency at Sick Kids Hospital right away as the metabolic department was expecting us. The drive was the longest, most silent, and fearsome journey I've ever experienced. My husband's eyes met mine, and I knew we would do whatever it took to protect our baby girl, but we felt terrified.

Newborn Screening Saved Her Life

At the emergency, a team of people took our daughter and began poking and prodding her. I remember being in a little room, flooded with geneticists, dietitians, metabolic doctors, and nurses. I was a mess and felt so helpless. I prayed it was a false positive. They quickly explained to us that they wanted to run some more tests to confirm a diagnosis for a rare metabolic condition called Glutaric Aciduria/Acidemia Type 1 (GA1). In the first twenty-four hours of life, all babies in Ontario are screened for GA1, along with twenty-eight other diseases.[2] I had never even heard of newborn screening (NBS). Although I had no idea what it was for specifically, I remember that nurse who took the drop of blood from my baby girl's heel after she was born, right before we brought her

2   Newborn Screening Ontario. (2017, October 27). Retrieved from http://www.newborn screening.ca

home for the first time. It was through NBS that my daughter's condition was diagnosed, and it saved her life.

Newborn screening saves thousands of lives every year, and I'm thankful every single day for this indescribable gift. It is the process of testing newborn babies for some serious, but treatable, conditions. The conditions newborn babies are screened for varies depending on province or state. According to Newborn Screening Ontario, hospitals now screen for twenty-nine diseases including metabolic diseases, cystic fibrosis, sickle cell anemia, PKU, and endocrine diseases. Babies with one of the tested diseases appear normal at birth, and without newborn screening, might not be identified before irreversible damage has occurred. Most of these babies will not have a family history of the disease. My husband and I are both carriers of GA1, but we had no idea.

We quickly learned that early identification of the disease allows treatment that can prevent severely devastating outcomes. It was challenging to find anything positive on the internet, but I kept searching and searching. It was one of the most difficult times in my life. I wanted to just curl up into a tiny ball, but I knew my daughter needed us to learn as much as possible. Children with GA1 who did not receive early treatment via NBS, most often suffered a crisis, also known as a metabolic stroke which left these angels in a wheelchair and typically non-verbal. Before GA1 was discovered in the late 1990s, it was believed to be late onset cerebral palsy or also referred to as locked-in syndrome. Fortunately, there is now technology such as the eye gaze system, to help these children communicate as they are all cognitively functioning at one hundred percent. All the families affected by GA1 are amazing warriors, battling the unknown, and sometimes what feels like the impossible. The research for this rare disease stops at six years old. After that, we celebrate graduating out of the high-risk zone and continue to monitor every single illness. From three months to thirty-six months is the highest risk for a GA1 child to have a metabolic stroke to the brain, also known as a crisis. We do everything in our power to avoid this, which could be triggered by something as common as a fever. These children are my superheroes, and these mama warriors are the ones who inspire me. Fortunately, there is a Facebook support group where we can follow each other's journeys, joys, challenges, and most importantly, lift each other up in the moments we need it most.

These mothers from all over the world are connecting, supporting, and rising up to be there for one another. The day I found this online support group, I felt a sense of hope and it changed my world.

Live In Love, Not Fear

After our daughter's diagnosis was confirmed, she was admitted to Sick Kids Hospital, Toronto where we were given a "crash course" on what GA1 was and the guidelines we had to follow to keep her healthy. We knew we had to avoid viruses at all costs. The next day, we were supposed to be taking her to our first family get together, which was now a threat to our baby girl. Everyone we knew had little kids who are like Petri dishes of germs. Her immune system is perfectly fine, but when a child with GA1 gets a cold, their bodies don't work as well. Children with metabolic conditions are often medically fragile. It was a tough time for us after our daughter's diagnosis. It was a turbulent ride going back and forth between exhaustion from sleeping at the hospital, to shock, to dealing with postpartum hormones, and then grief. My vision, of what I envisioned motherhood to be, had been completely altered.

The real challenge was to remain positive, hopeful, and powerful in the middle of it all. Often, our automatic panic button is in overdrive and we can be swept away by fear. I was definitely in a complete state of fear and blinked back tears as the doctors continued to explain that people with metabolic conditions have a defective gene that results in an enzyme deficiency. I asked them if there was a cure, and how rare it is, and he let me know that 1 in 100,000 children are affected and this is a condition she will have for life. Sick Kids Hospital had two other cases of GA1. It hit me like a lightning bolt, despite how helpless I felt, I had to learn as much as I could to protect my daughter. I soaked up all the information like a sponge and became obsessed with trying to understand it all. My daughter's body can't break down protein properly. Specifically, her body is unable to break down the amino acids lysine, hydroxylysine, and tryptophan.[3] A toxic substance of glutaric acid builds up in her body which could cause a stroke to the basal ganglia part of

---

3 2017, November 4. National Center for Advancing Translational Sciences. Retrieved from https://rarediseases.info.nih.gov/diseases/6522/glutaric-acidemia-type-i

her brain. She is at high risk of having a metabolic stroke at any sign of illness until she is three years of age. The common cold could put her in the hospital. The risk decreases significantly once she turns six-years-old, as that part of the brain is fully developed. However, there are still so many unknowns about this condition as it has only been considered treatable since 2006.

Our New Reality

I had multiple questions swirling around in my mind at full speed. *What if I make a mistake? How am I going to do this? What if I fail?* I think a lot of parenting is about believing in your abilities and trusting that you've got this. I learned that it's not what happens to us but how we choose to respond. Often, adversity will be an opportunity to gain a new perspective if you allow it. I tried to remind myself that out of great difficulties, there can be miracles. I also thought that I would be the person to show and teach my daughter how to be brave and believe in herself. I was wrong. In fact, it is she who has taught me these things on a whole new level.

She began her medications at six-days-old and takes them three times a day and even though she's only sixteen-months-old, she takes them herself like a champ. She will be on these meds for life, along with a protein (lysine) restricted diet and special medical formula. We measure everything on a scale. It's complicated because pretty much everything we eat has protein in it. Even watermelon has protein and needs to be measured so she doesn't consume too much lysine. Most important is the illness management protocol, which involves IV fluids at any sign of illness, fever, diarrhea, or lack of appetite. The IV fluids provide extra sugars and hydration, both of which are vital to protect her brain. This prevents her body from breaking down her own protein when the demand for energy has increased. Preventing this catabolic state is what prevents the toxins from building up in her brain. She had weekly appointments at Sick Kids Hospital for blood work and now they are every couple of months. Her most recent hospitalization involved eight attempts before finding a final IV spot. My daughter inspires me so much and her bravery makes me stronger. She has been through a lot, but continues to radiate endless love and light. Every time we are there,

I ask myself, *What can I do to protect her more?* or *What should I be advocating for right now?* It's often hard for me to fully trust the doctors and nurses. None of us are experts in GA1. It's the absolute epitome of lifelong learning. Right now, she can have four grams of protein a day. We have to keep daily logs of her food and medical formula intake. Luckily, as she grows older, her protein allowance will increase. These are all positives as they keep our daughter safe. She is thriving and it definitely keeps us moving forward.

Strength From My Soul Sisters And Mothers

I have learned to live in love and not fear. It definitely took some time, as I had to mourn certain expectations and learn to embrace this new journey. The day my daughter was diagnosed, my husband inspired me by saying, "We will not let GA1 defeat us and we need to shower away any negativity or fear." That is just what we did and we have survived so much together this past year. My own incredible mother also gave me powerful advice when I was feeling less than confident to handle everything. She said, "You can do this because she's your daughter and you are her protector." I began to focus on what could go right rather than the things that could go wrong. Although very few people understood this rare condition, I felt compelled to explain this rare condition to anyone who would listen. I was very fortunate and had a few friends who indeed got it. They helped by checking in, listening, and reminding me to stay positive. These friends are also incredible mothers and I will forever be grateful for their support when I needed it most. A special thank you to my friend Tia, who was our very first visitor during our first hospitalization. I remember the nurses telling me someone was waiting at the registration desk. I wondered who it was, and as I slowly walked out of isolation, I saw my incredibly thoughtful and selfless good friend, Tia. It brought tears to my eyes and I will forever remember that hug because I have never needed one more. She couldn't come and see my daughter because we were in isolation, but she left us with some homemade muffins and hope. She reminded me that we were in an incredible place surrounded by miracles. As mothers and women warriors, we all need to connect and embrace each other during the challenges of this journey called motherhood. Not only is it about reframing our thinking or rediscovering feelings that empower and uplift us. We need to reach out to others to help guide us, teach us, and then take these lessons and share them with others. I genuinely believe the Universe is always working for us and if we learn to listen to the subtle signs, then we are reminded that we are not alone. We need to lean on each other, inspire each other, and empower one another. This is what can show our children that they too can be unstoppable and resilient in the face of adversity. There are villages of mama warriors that surround us, and I believe that there's always an opportunity that can be discovered from a difficult situation.

Raising A Medically Fragile Child

Adjusting to this new lifestyle of raising a medically fragile child has definitely been a process. It means we have decided to avoid taking her to public places where people are often sick. Daycare is not an option. Neither are airplanes or traveling right now. Our daughter has never been to a mall, a grocery store, or a public play space. We prefer to socialize outdoors with her, but cold and flu season is the scariest. We sanitize constantly and hand hygiene is of utmost importance to us. We had to miss Christmas and other various family get-togethers because of someone having a cold or some virus. Being new parents and having to avoid family and friends due to illness constantly can be very isolating. When my husband or I are feeling unwell, we wear a mask at all times, or leave home and stay somewhere else, until we are no longer a threat to our daughter. Playdates can be dangerous as toddlers are often carriers of viruses even when they appear well. Birthday parties are a challenge. She's allowed four grams of protein a day and all of her food has to be measured continuously. Birthday cake, pizza, and ice cream all have too much protein for her to have right now. Despite these new ways of living, I am eternally grateful and humbled to know my daughter has a chance to live a normal and healthy life.

Despite all of our precautions, she has had nine hospitalizations in the first year of her life because of illness. These were extremely emotional and hard, but visitors always put a smile on our faces. My sister always reminds me that our daughter is a fighter and has been an amazing source of support. My daughter is a happy, healthy, and strong toddler who lights up every room she is in. Life with a rare condition is a unique journey and her determined spirit and fearless nature makes us braver and more hopeful with each new moment. However, raising a medically fragile child has you constantly thinking about what germs you are possibly bringing home. If I have been in a crowded public place, I will shower and change my clothes before holding my daughter. We sanitize our phones and wash our hands immediately upon entering the house. Everyone that comes over mustn't be around anyone sick and must wash their hands and sanitize before touching our daughter. Our family doctor always lets our daughter have the first appointment of the day to avoid sick people. The metabolic doctors are on speed dial in case of illness twenty-four hours a day. This is life with a medically fragile child, and I wouldn't change it for the world. Motherhood has shown me what I am capable of, and being able to nurture our daughter's progress is pure magic. Every single day and every second with our daughter is a gift. She is our bright light and little GA1 warrior who reminds us to be fearless in the face of adversity and to dance every day.

Unstoppable

Every milestone she achieves magnifies our gratitude, our joy, and our hopes. Every day that she spends at home and away from the hospital is a victory. Each moment she laughs and engages with another child without getting sick is a relief. Looking into my daughter's innocent eyes, I can see her fierce determination and her unstoppable spirit which makes all of this possible. Her power is confidence, her power is resilience, and her power is love. I strive to be present and grateful in every moment, which is not always easy. I try to remember to embrace every single second of motherhood, because often, we feel so exhausted and lose the ability to be present. We accomplish what needs to be done and we live in love rather than fear. To feel powerful when faced with adversity can take time and healing. One of the doctors gave me great advice. She said, "You need to remember to enjoy your baby." In that moment, I realized that I was so consumed with my daughter's meds, diet, illness management protocols, and how many bottles of medical formula she had consumed in a day, that I forgot to let myself live and be present within each beautiful and messy moment as a new mother. I was given this remarkable gift and needed to treasure every single day. I have this fantastic opportunity to watch my child grow.

Whether motherhood carries excitement, joy, sorrow, painful decisions, tender love, or confusion, it is our destiny. It is my purpose to keep our angel safe, advocate for our little GA1 warrior, and educate the world around her about her rare needs. Whether you can relate to my journey or not, we were all given a unique treasure. Motherhood isn't always glamorous but we need to continue to be our child's protector, advocate, and their blanket of love. To show them that they too can be unstoppable and can do anything is the ultimate gift we can give them. The possibilities are endless and there is this love we feel with every fiber of our being for our child. It is the most motivating and powerful force that can give us a strength we didn't even know we had.

~ To Sage, may you always love yourself unconditionally, share your light and expect miracles. You truly are golden. To my husband with love: Thank you for being a strong light in our little girl's life and for supporting my aspirations. For my amazing family and the extraordinary women in my life, thank you for being my soul tribe.

8

BOTTLE OR BREAST, FED IS BEST!

by Melissa Smith

"No matter what you decide, own it like the fierce mama you are."

Melissa Smith

Melissa is a mom to three beautiful children and a devoted wife to an amazing husband. She knew from a young age that she yearned to be a wife and mother. Before starting a family, Melissa studied health and recreation, strength training, and physical education. She has been involved in teaching and strength training teens and women, and is also an advocate for the advancement of women in sport and physical activity. Melissa traveled abroad and obtained her teaching certification while residing in Australia. She is a creative soul, enjoys the sun and surf, and has a great love for the outdoors. As an individual living with type 1 diabetes for twenty-four years, she is an avid supporter of the Juvenile Diabetes Research Foundation. She is an energetic and passionate leader who has had a successful career in retail management. As an ambitious, independent, and aspiring mompreneur, Melissa enjoys living with a positive work-life balance and aims to be successful through her business. She plans on sharing her creative designs, and looks forward to participating in trade shows, and starting a blog in the upcoming year to share her fitness journey after having three children. As someone with an outgoing and caring personality, she enjoys meeting people and nurturing relationships. Melissa's focus is to spend more time with her family and return to her passions of health and wellness while getting involved with her community. She is looking forward to surrounding herself with strong entrepreneurial individuals as she embarks on the next chapter of her life.

www.youniqueproducts.com/MelisSmith
www.healthymommy.ca
fb: Younique Makeup by Melissa

"Your top job as a new parent is to love your baby like crazy.
After showering her with affection, your next two important jobs
are to feed her and to calm her when she cries."
~ Dr. Harvey Karp

I SPENT NINE MONTHS FEELING as though I was as big as a cow and then quite literally, became the cow. I hadn't realized how challenging breastfeeding would be until I decided to do so. It is a huge commitment, a ton of work, and requires a lot of support. I am not someone who will tell you that "breast is best" for your baby. Each woman needs to consider what feels right for them, their baby and family at the time; whether that is breast, formula or a combination of both. The message from The Fed is Best Foundation is, "Mothers shouldn't be shamed and babies go hungry, simply because breast milk isn't always a viable option." A happy and healthy baby and mama is the most important thing. No matter what you decide, own it like the fierce mama you are and know you've got this!

Commitment

I breastfed three children (currently breastfeeding), and each baby has been a different experience with different challenges. The one thing constant with all three of my children was that they were Neonatal Intensive Care Unit (NICU) babies, so I was separated from them shortly after birth. Through three high-risk pregnancies due to type 1 diabetes and insulin pump therapy, each of my babies required support with sugar levels by intravenous therapy and were fed with a tube that goes through the nose down into the stomach (NG tube).

When my first son Christopher was born, my labor was induced, it was long and I ended up in the operating room for support with delivery. My baby was whisked away covered in monitors, CPAP breathing machine, and needed to have an IV right away. Once out of recovery, a lactation consultant explained everything there was to know about breastfeeding in a matter of thirty minutes. I felt so overwhelmed. However, she was very reassuring which gave me the confidence to try. I learned that I would need to pump since my baby was not with me to feed. She came back with a big archaic looking machine which was a breast pump, and assisted with fitting the horns and placement on my breasts. I remember looking at this device in the corner of the room and laughing to myself while I sat alone in my room at night.

Every three hours, I would make my way from my ward to the NICU to visit with my baby. He would need his vitals done and to be changed within his isolette incubator. Then with the nurse's assistance, I would sit and hold the NG tube to feed him formula as my milk had not yet come in and he needed the sugar. Before having my son, I wasn't aware that there was a possibility that he would be classified as "failure to thrive" without medical/nutritional intervention. It wasn't for lack of trying; I felt exhausted and the pumping became so frustrating after several days. I would dutifully pump every three hours, only to end up with a tiny pea size drop of colostrum in the bottle when I was finished. The nurses would cheer me on, but I just wanted to cry. There were so many times I thought about giving up and that this was all too much for me. Then I would hold my little boy in my arms and I decided that I wanted to do this for him. Mothers seem to have an innate desire to nourish their babies once they are born. I had many friends and family who were having children at the same time, some of them also breastfed while others had thriving formula fed babies. It is essential to decide what works best for the whole family. Some women formula feed due to issues with their nipples, milk supply, or medications that were not safe to take while breastfeeding. While others wanted their bodies to feel like their own again or they wanted or needed help from others to feed so they could rest. Afterall, it does take a village to feed a baby.

Work

As weeks and months passed, the pumping became less and less and the nursing became easier. I loved breastfeeding; it was such a rewarding experience even though it was a lot of work. I still needed to pump since we were giving our baby formula in the evening before bed. Initially, I was concerned about combining nursing with formula feeding but learned that other mothers fed their babies in similar ways. Feeding in this way afforded me the opportunity to have others help with feeding. It meant that we always had milk in the fridge and I was able to have some much-needed mommy time too. These times weren't always glamorous and a good sense of humor comes in handy when breastfeeding. There were so many changes happening to my body. It's incredible how breasts fill up with milk and how swollen and leaky they become if not nursing or pumping.

I had the pleasure of experiencing two wedding mishaps. We were having a great evening full of dinner, dancing, and enjoying the company of great friends. However, when we sat down to enjoy the late night buffet, I noticed that my shirt felt wet. When I arrived at the bathroom, I discovered that both the breast pads in my bra were fully soaked and my breast milk was leaking all over my top. Thankfully, I was wearing black and the rest of the guests were none the wiser. We ended up leaving the event early due to my wardrobe malfunction. When we got in the car, I pulled out my pump; plugged in the battery pack and on the highway home, cuddled beneath my husband's dress coat, I pumped two full bottles of milk. We smiled and laughed about the scenario the entire way. Next time, I knew I would need to pump sooner and always have extra breast pads handy. Lesson learned, or so I had thought.

The second wedding mishap occurred at an overnight wedding out of town, a big step for a first time mom who is breastfeeding. We took a bus with other party guests from the hotel to the venue, about 45 minutes away. I realized about four hours into the event that I had forgotten my pump at the hotel and we were going to be here for at least eight hours. My breasts became heavy as rocks while sitting at the table for dinner. It became more and more unbearable as the time passed, and it felt as though my breast would burst. So, there I found myself in a beautiful dress at a gorgeous venue, in a bathroom stall, straddling a toilet and squeezing my breasts into it. I came back to the table and leaned over to my husband and whispered to him, "Jeremy, you wouldn't believe what I just did." I confessed to him, and the rest of the table of close friends and we all roared. Hand expressing milk isn't the most efficient way to express milk, but it certainly works in a pinch. I made several trips to the bathroom that night and it became a night that we would never forget and we would reminisce for years to come.

We were pregnant a second time but sadly experienced a miscarriage. During my third pregnancy, my body changed rapidly. Weight gain was immediate and my breasts were enlarged very early on. The nipple on my right breast had become leathery and hard. I had discussed my concerns with my medical team, and they determined it was due to changes in pregnancy hormones. My breast had already started leaking during the third trimester. My body just seemed to know what to do and was gearing up to feed another baby. It was reassuring to know that I wasn't going to experience all the challenges I faced with our first. Little did I know that I was soon to experience a different set of challenges. I had a routine ultrasound and my doctor made the decision that my baby would be healthier if delivered the very next day and five weeks early. Labor was induced and our little guy ended up being in distress, so we made the decision to have a c-section. When Benjamin, our rainbow baby, was born, he was assessed and taken to the NICU. I couldn't believe that we were experiencing everything that we had with our first child, all over again. This time the sugar took longer to adjust and required more intravenous therapy. I began pumping very soon after recovery and was able to pump full bottles after only a short period of time. *Moo, right!* My fridge and freezer had quickly turned into a milk storage center and we had even joked about being able to feed the entire NICU. All kidding aside, we had considered donating breast milk. The Milk Bank of Ontario collects, regulates, and distributes donor milk to hospital NICUs for preterm babies with low birth weight, where mothers' milk is not a viable option. Pasteurized donor milk assists in saving the lives of critically ill, hospitalized babies.

I was discharged from the hospital after a week, but our baby wasn't able to feed on his own due to being premature and fed with an NG tube. I would drive our first son to daycare and then go to the hospital and sit with our newest addition from 9am to 4pm until it was time to pick up our firstborn from daycare. Jeremy would go and visit in the evenings. Our baby was eventually transferred to another hospital during the time he was still learning to feed. It was the change we needed since I was able to work with the nursing and lactation team to get our baby to latch and nurse well before being discharged. Throughout this time, my nipple had never corrected itself. I couldn't pump or nurse well on that side. It became raw, cracked and bleeding. I needed to take time not using that breast until it healed. I continued to experience difficulties with that breast throughout the year and it was painful when nursing. My other breast made up for the difference and I was still able to nurse despite not being able to get as much milk from that side but shortly after weaning my nipple had returned to normal.

My daughter, Aliyah, was born a few months ago, and we decided that we would like to breastfeed again. During my fourth pregnancy, my nipple on my right breast did the same thing it had before. It was disappointing to know that I was going to have to endure the pain and challenges again. Our girl ended up being the easiest for delivery (scheduled c-section) and recovery in the NICU. However, she has been the most challenging to feed and the slowest to gain weight. I pumped as soon as I could and I was happy and surprised that I was able to pump so much so quickly. That changed. I was pumping every three hours while visiting her in the NICU, exactly as I had done with our first two babies. I would pump for twenty minutes and end up with a pea-sized drop of milk in the bottle. I was so tired and becoming frustrated with pumping and it had only been a couple of days. The next morning I got myself ready and headed to the NICU. I formula fed her with an NG tube and rather than returning her to her isolette, I sat with her and enjoyed skin to skin. Up until now, there had not been many opportunities to hold my daughter, let alone have skin to skin contact. So, I sat with her for hours and just enjoyed our warm bodies against each other. Again, we were transferred to another hospital; she recovered her sugar levels quickly and was off IV shortly after arriving at the new hospital. When I sat down to pump at her bedside, I was astonished at the difference. I was able to pump two full bottles. I was also experiencing terrible engorgement. I stood in front of the mirror, and stared at these breasts the size of cantaloupes and heavy as bricks, and laughed. They would spontaneously start leaking. I would get out of the shower and be grabbing for towels to press on the two fountains spraying from my breasts. You haven't lived until you have squirted your husband with milk from your breast as he laughs at you hysterically scrambling for towels, breast pads, receiving blankets, or anything you could get your hands on quickly. A lactation consultant visited me at the new hospital and was amazing support and a wealth of knowledge.

Support

I discussed with my lactation consultant about my leathery nipple and explained how much I suffered nursing my second son as well as my engorgement concerns. She showed me all sorts of great things to try to solve the "nipple issue." I was thrilled to learn that she had just dealt with another mama who had a similar issue. It is so reassuring to hear that I was not alone. I started putting nipple cream on before and after pumping, used a larger size horn on that breast, and learned how to make a "nipple donut" out of facial tissue so that the cream didn't wipe off onto the breast pads right away. Amazingly my nipple has returned to normal. If only I had bumped into this woman three years ago. She also suggested cold cabbage for my engorgement. I had heard about using it in the past but had never tried it because it seemed so ridiculous. She brought some cold leaves to me and helped me stuff my bra with them. I couldn't believe that I felt relief almost immediately. If you haven't tried the cabbage experience for yourself, I highly recommend it.

We decided to work on feeding our daughter with a bottle so that we could go home since we had two little guys who were missing mama. The nurses at this hospital were fabulous cheerleaders. It felt like a real tribe of mamas supporting me and cheering me on. Once we were home, my sweet daughter was gaining weight, but I was having a difficult time with latching at the breast. I wasn't able to get a big open mouth to put the baby on the breast; she would always purse her lips and be hanging off the end of my nipples. I would have to take her off to reposition and try the latch again, and again. She would click while nursing and swallow air causing a great amount of gas and colic. We spent weeks trying to master the latch and work out her gas concerns. I reached out to resources by phone and visits with my family doctor and nurse to support me through the process. There have been many times when I thought that I couldn't bear another minute breastfeeding. At almost twelve weeks old, we have finally got it figured out.

I have learned over the years how important it is to ask for help. It doesn't make you any less of a mom or a woman. We have to build each other up and support each other whether we are nursing or formula feeding our sweet babes. There will be people who judge you for formula feeding or nursing in public or for hundreds of other reasons as you raise your children. Be fierce, Mama, and do what is best for you, your baby, and family. Agree to disagree. I do my research by reaching out to professionals or my tribe of mamas to help me make the best decisions possible for my children. Ultimately, these decisions are yours and as long as you and your baby are safe and healthy stick to your guns. I have been so thankful to have the help of my immediate family, my husband's family, a large extended family, and close friends. Aliyah is feeding beautifully and is such a happy little girl. I enjoy the time I get to bond with her and it has become such a rewarding experience and similar to how I enjoyed feeding my boys. Enjoy feeding your baby. No matter the method of feeding, fed is always best.

It takes a village to raise children and support is so important. I am so grateful for all the support I have, especially my mother. She is my biggest supporter, my sounding board, and my extra set of hands. My beautiful mama has been at my side through everything, high-risk pregnancies, and intense deliveries, babies in the NICU, my recoveries, doctor's appointments, late nights, and early mornings and everything in between. She is the superhero that I aspire to be. She is always telling me that I am such a good mama, but I'd like to think it's only because I had such a good teacher.

~ Many thanks to Jeremy, the best husband in the world and my beautiful children, Christopher, Benjamin, and Aliyah for inspiring me to follow my dreams.

9

I REALLY THOUGHT I'D BE THE MOTHERHOOD EXCEPTION OF LOVE AT FIRST SIGHT

by Sherri Marie Gaudet

"A mother's intuition about her child is the strongest around."

Sherri Marie Gaudet

Sherri Marie believes you should always live in the present moment. She is positive to a fault and will always find a way to make even the most boring task fun. She is all about finding the good in even the worst of situations. She loves to have fun but understands there is a time and place for everything in life. Sherri Marie loves being around her friends, both new and old. She can walk into a crowded room full of strangers, and within a few minutes, can be found chatting away forming new friendships. She has always been one who sets her mind to something and, no matter how hard it is, will find a way to accomplish it.

Although she didn't always know what she wanted to do when she grew up, Sherri Marie always knew that she wanted to be someone who helped people. She was always a risk taker, often doing before thinking. She always believed that nothing in the world was impossible, doing her best work when the odds were stacked against her. Sherri Marie tried out various career paths during her twenties before finally realizing that her talents were best spent helping others as an entrepreneur and business leader.

Sherri Marie is a national market developer / recruiter. She strives to help people believe in themselves and design lives they love.

www.lifestyleofsherrimarie.com
ig: @Lifestyleofsherrimarie
fb: sherrimarie

"Being a mother is learning about strengths you didn't know you had, and dealing with fears you didn't know existed."
~ Linda Wooten

THEY ALWAYS SAY, from the minute you place your eyes on your child, your life will never again be the same. They say that the love you will instantly feel is unlike anything you have ever felt before. Up until the minute I saw my son's big blue eyes, I have to admit, I thought I would be the exception to this. To say I was not ready or excited to become a mom, just might be the understatement of the century. Here I was worried about postpartum depression when I was experiencing prepartum depression hell. To be honest, I was in denial about even becoming a mom the entire time I was pregnant with my son.

July 19, 2007, at 6:11pm, my world as I knew it changed forever as I locked eyes with my son for the very first time. He was completely perfect in every way possible. I couldn't believe he was mine, even more so, I couldn't believe I had doubted if I would love him. My son came out looking healthy to me in every way possible, the cutest little peanut and when I say little, I mean little.

You see, I had been struck with the flu during my pregnancy at a critical time in his development. Doctors say a week earlier, and I would have had a miscarriage. A week later, and it wouldn't have affected him at all. But unfortunately, the virus struck me during this delicate window and affected my son's growth. The night my son was born was so surreal to me. Being tiny at only two pounds and 6 ounces, he looked small, yes, but his lungs were strong and healthy. He was very alert and responsive to everything. Yet, all the doctors and nurses were telling me differently. We have a problem, they told me. Your son has contracted a virus which has and will always handicap him. I remember just holding him, and nothing they were saying to me was even registering. I think they realized they were not getting anywhere with me that night because they finally stopped. They did insist on keeping my son in the Neonatal Intensive Care Unit (NICU) that night, and quite honestly, at that point, I was so exhausted I didn't argue with them.

The morning after my son was born; I was up early and ready to see him. I couldn't get down to that NICU soon enough. I was less than impressed when I showed up at 7am and was told I wouldn't be able to see him until after the doctor's rounds were complete at 10am. I might have been young and had no business speaking up, but that was my son, and nobody was going to keep him from me. I asked to speak with the head nurse on duty and explained to her that making me wait until 10am was not an option. She was so sweet and told me to please hold on a few minutes. She came back and let me know that the doctors had just finished the rounds and they wanted to sit down with me and talk. She asked if I had any other family at the hospital that wanted to sit in on the meeting. I said, "Of course, I have a room full of them, let me get them."

I can remember every detail of that meeting, start to finish, right down to where people were sitting, and even what people were wearing. What can I say, I have a crazy memory. It's a blessing and a curse, trust me. I remember the head doctor on duty at the NICU leading the meeting; she did not mince her words at all. This doctor got straight to the point as soon as the meeting started, beginning with, "You have to realize how critically ill your son is and there is ZERO hope for him. I am 100% sure that your son will NEVER be a normal boy as he will not walk or talk. He will never feel your touch or be able to touch you. He will not be able to do any of the things regular children do. I am not giving you a possible scenario; I am telling you with certainty that your son will never do any of these things." I did not let her say another word; I stood right up and walked over to the doctor as she was mid-sentence. I cut her off and told her that she was 100% wrong, that she did not know who she was talking to or what kind of strength my son had. I told her that my son would PROVE her wrong. He was going to be okay, and nothing she or anyone else told me would change my mind. She looked right at me with her cold, dark, brown eyes and said to me that she was extremely educated, well known, and highly respected as a doctor and so I should listen to her. At this point, I had enough of her. I told her that she was fired as my son's doctor and that when she looked back on this case, she was going to realize that she had just made the biggest mistake of her career. I told her that she needed to learn from this because in my world there is no such thing as zero hope. There was a team of doctors in that meeting who all looked like deer in headlights after my conversation with the head doctor. I looked around that room at each of them and told them all they just witnessed the most valuable lesson of their careers. The truth was I truly believed what I was saying with all my heart and soul. Call it who I am. Call it a mother's intuition. Call it whatever you want, but nobody was going to tell me my son had zero hope for living a healthy life because of a virus.

The next doctor, who replaced the first doctor, explained to me that because of when I had become sick during my pregnancy, it did affect my son and that we had to treat it with a very dangerous drug called Ghanziclovear for six weeks. I was so nervous about giving him such a potent drug being only days old, but my gut instinct told me to give it to him. It was a long six weeks. There were a few setbacks with one blood transfusion, but overall, it went really well. I spent every second in that NICU during his treatment and oversaw every single thing with his medical care. I would not allow the nurses or doctors to do much. He was my son, and I was going to take care of him, nobody else. I pushed the limits as a mom for sure, but isn't that what moms are supposed to do? One thing I had researched was music and how beneficial it was for developing brains, so I got him an iPod. Looking back ten years later, wow, that iPod was huge and so dated compared to what we have now. But it got the job done.

The happiest day was when he finished his medicine and was able to come home. I don't think anyone ran out of that NICU quicker than we did, and there was absolutely no looking back for us. They offered me all these different groups for NICU parents, I am sure they were very beneficial for many moms but I wanted no part of them. That first doctor had put such a negative, traumatizing taste in my mouth, I couldn't get out of that NICU fast enough and I just wanted to put that part of our life behind us. However, it wasn't that easy for me. The first doctor had told me that by the time my son turned five years of age, he would be a completely abnormal child. I never once in my gut believed her, yet it was always in the back of my mind. Each year that went by as we celebrated birthday after birthday, instead of just being excited for him to be another year older, I would be ecstatic that we were another year closer to being five. I just never could get her words out of my head, and yet I never believed them.

I can still remember every last detail like it was yesterday and not six years ago. I can remember standing in my salon laughing with everyone not having really a care in the world, even though my son was at a hearing appointment. You see, it never even dawned on me that it would be anything but routine, which is why I didn't take the day off work to take him. He had been suffering from what we thought was an ear infection. He had just recently returned home from a trip to Florida and let's be serious here for a minute, who doesn't get sick from traveling? I remember my phone ringing when I was mid-laugh, it was my dad. My dad always calls me "Sher." It is only when I am in trouble or it's something serious that he calls me Sherri and he never starts a conversation seriously. My dad is one of those people who are funny and goofy by nature. He doesn't try to be, but he has that presence. However, he is also able to take charge when something is serious. "Sherri we have a problem, Brady has lost his hearing..." My entire world came to a screeching halt. Everything from his NICU days came rushing back to me; it was the most overwhelming feeling in the world. Later we would find out they were completely unrelated, but in that moment, it was so scary. I remember being mid-laugh and then everything around me going completely black. I was lucky enough to be around some awesome people that day, one of my friends drove my car home, I can't remember much about that drive, but I do remember him looking me in the eyes and telling me, "It will be ok." I remember walking in my house and nothing felt the same, I felt like the person I was when I had left home just a few hours ago was gone, I felt like everything in my life had just been taken away. One of my friends was staying at my house for a few months and asked me, "What can I do? What do you need?" I looked at her blankly and said, "Make all of this a really bad dream." She is more religious than I, and so, she did the only thing she knew how to do. She created a "prayer" group online and invited everyone she could think of. Within just a few minutes, that group was filled with nothing but positivity from both people I knew and didn't know. As I sat there hysterically sobbing, I kept getting notifications on my phone from this group and after about a half hour I was like, *Okay we got this, and will fight through this, crying won't change this, and isn't being proactive.*

I got out my phone and googled the hearing specialist in Rhode Island and asked for the office manager. I told her, didn't ask, but told her that I was bringing my son there in an hour and I was not leaving until we were seen. Now, mind you, I had never been there before, I had absolutely NO business in doing that, but I was persistent in my call and she told me to bring him in. I dried my tears, picked up my son, and off to Providence we went. I walked in with him, and they couldn't have been more helpful to us. They took us right into a room and did the evaluation which did confirm his hearing loss. The doctor explained to me that it was nothing I had done, he had merely caught a virus and it had settled in his ear, she looked at me and told me he would be okay. I remember looking her in the eyes and saying, "Yes, I know he will be." The doctors told me this couldn't have happened at a better time; he was old enough that his speech was fully developed, yet young enough that his body will compensate for this loss. But they did recommend hearing aids; I did not agree with that, as I am more about natural healing, not to mention, I remember the boy in my elementary school with hearing aids and how much he was tormented. No, that was not going to be my son. I left that office and felt like going there was such a huge mistake. I didn't know it at the time, but it wasn't a mistake. This diagnosis was going to teach me the biggest lessons in life and motherhood. I went home that night, and had my parents take my son for overnight, while my closest friends came over offering me my favorites: wine and pizza. And yet, I didn't want either of those two things. I just wanted to curl up in a ball and cry. I felt like all my hopes and dreams I had for being a mom were gone. I allowed myself to cry myself to sleep that night and the next morning when I woke up I knew I had to tackle this head-on.

After a lot of pressure from a lot of people in my life, I did get my son hearing aids; it was the first time in my journey as a mom where I did something, which at the time, didn't feel like the right decision intuitively. Looking back now, I think I was worried about how it would affect him. I was concerned that children would be cruel. I was afraid that he wouldn't be the same child he was before he caught this virus. I couldn't have been more wrong. As mothers, we always think we are supposed to teach our children all about life, but really, they are the ones sometimes who are imparting life lessons to us. Before my son caught this virus, I had planned on having his entire first-grade class over for an Easter egg hunt that weekend and although everyone told me to cancel, my son asked me to have it anyway, so I did. Seeing him interact with his friends, I knew for the first time, we were going to be okay, he was still the same child. This virus he caught, it didn't destroy him, in many ways, it created him. It made me a better mom and in many ways, a better person.

As mothers, we always have this vision of how we think life should be or how it is supposed to unravel, but is that even realistic? I mean, let's be serious here for a minute. How often does life really play out exactly how we plan? We want to keep our children in these bubbles and never have them experience hard times, but what I have learned is that they are more resilient than we would ever give them credit for. If you were to meet my son, you would NEVER know he lost his hearing; he is just like every single child his age, he is always the leader in whatever it is that he does. I remember a few years ago, we were at karate and a child asked him what was in his ears. I instantly felt sick to my stomach, yet my son answered with such posture and confidence. "They help me hear better, aren't they cool?" It was a moment in my life I will never forget. I have always believed that the way we present something to our children and the vibe we give off, directly affects how they handle things themselves. I have always presented any bump along the journey of life to my son as being positive, regardless if most would view it as a negative. It is how I have always lived my life and something that was very important for me to instill in him. I truly believe in my heart that is one of the main reasons he has handled his bumps along his life journey so flawlessly.

I am happy to say my son is now ten years old and one happy, smart, and well-rounded person. My sister who is currently in medical school was at a conference last year and bumped into that first doctor who told me that my son had zero chance of surviving at all. The doctor remembered my son and myself vividly and was very surprised to hear how things had played out in my son's life. This just goes to show that doctors, as intelligent as they are, do make mistakes sometimes. Most of all, when all else fails, a mother's intuition about her child is the strongest healing force there is.

~ I dedicate my chapter to my amazing son, Brady,
we don't have it all together, but together, we have it all.

10

RUN TOWARDS
THE ROAR

by Jessica Janzen Olstad

"Live differently
- live on purpose
with boldness
and joy."

Jessica Janzen Olstad

Jessica Janzen Olstad, along with her husband, Hot Ronnie, is the co-founder of the Love for Lewiston Foundation, an inspirational speaker, and an influencer of joy. Hot Ronnie and Jess are mom and dad to Swayzie Grace and Lewiston James (who is dancing in Heaven). They desire more kids and are trusting God to fill their family with more healthy children whichever way they come.

This farm girl, now urban city dweller loves a good pair of heels and heading out to explore a new restaurant or city. Jess ditched her corporate gig and the 9 -5 grind to live her most authentic, bold, and joyful life. She believes that her story has a purpose and has committed her life to sharing her testimony to encourage others to get unstuck and truly start living. In addition to blogging and doing things that make her heart soar, Jessica has developed and designed a clothing line made locally in her hometown of Calgary, Canada to help raise funds and awareness for the Love for Lewiston Foundation. Her least favorite question is… "So what do you do?" As on any given day, she is mopping up another mess and cleaning the kitchen for the millionth time, or dreaming up her next design for her clothing line, or writing a chapter for her own book which is set to be released in late fall of 2018.

She takes pleasure in the small things such as good coffee, shoe shopping, getting a good sweat on, and soaking up the sunshine by the water.

www.jessicajanzen.ca | www.loveforlewiston.ca
Ig: @jsjanzen | @loveforlewiston

"... Most people die at twenty-five and aren't buried
until they're seventy-five. Don't let that happen to you.
Don't let your soul stop growing and don't give in even
if your stomach is growling. Your greatest days are still to come.
I dare you to believe that the days will come where
what you are most scared of right now will be included
in your highlight reel as a triumphant victory. The only way
to truly live is to run toward the roar."
~ Levi Lusko

YOU KNOW WHEN YOU FEEL OFF AND WONDER, *Why am I feeling this way? Could it be that I am pregnant again?* I mean, come on, we use the pull out method. Hot Ronnie (my husband, who is now known as Hot Ronnie) has used this method many times and assured me it has always worked. Regardless of how confident he feels about it working, I am not as convinced and decided to pee on a stick. There have just been too many signs pointing to the fact that another baby is on the way. I knew it wasn't from lack of sleep as our daughter who was just about five months old was sleeping a solid twelve hours through the night. I felt rested.

How could I think I was pregnant?! *We were so not ready for this, definitely not ready to welcome another babe, we were barely getting by, I wasn't working, and Hot Ronnie was a partner in a small business start-up that had to pour every last bit back into the business. I needed to get back to some type of work, and I wouldn't even qualify for another mat leave.*

So there I went and peed on a stick and seconds later, I discover baby number two was on the way. Don't get me wrong, we wanted a second babe, heck, we wanted like three more! But this was a little faster than we had planned or were ready for. We were told by several doctors that we most likely wouldn't be able to have children of our own with my messed up body. Boy, were they ever wrong. I am beyond grateful for my fertility and count my blessings. I know far too many women who struggle to get pregnant and may never have that chance in their lifetime, so as much as this pregnancy came out of left field and was a total shocker, I counted my blessings. Fast forward nine months later.

It's May 25, 2016, and just two days before my due date, the contractions started. I forced myself to go to the gym earlier that night so I could walk – it was more of a waddle and every ten minutes, I would stop to pee, but I got in over an hour of walking. I was determined to have this baby early. So, at 2am when the contractions started, I got up, grabbed myself a bowl of cereal and watched an episode of Fixer Upper that was already recorded on my PVR. I waited at home as a second-time-mom would before I couldn't take the contractions anymore. I curled my hair, did my makeup, and was determined to look good and impress the medical staff with how I had this delivery. I had, legit, just been at this very hospital thirteen months ago, so I remembered and knew all too well what to expect.

When we arrived at the hospital, I was already 6cm dilated and got escorted in. I let them know my plan and how it would all go down. I didn't walk in with a binder of a birth plan, I just knew it was going to be quick and I didn't want someone stroking the side of my arm telling me how awesome it was going to be. That's what the nurse did with Swayzie, our daughter, and I hated it. Nothing about having that much pain felt awesome. Once you have them on your chest, however, it is everything – but the lead up to that moment was not awesome for me.

The game plan went like this: I would ask them to break my water with the long crochet hook and soon after that, I would fully dilate and the baby would be here not too long after that. I remember telling the doctor that morning that I was glad she had eaten her breakfast and was fueling up because when this baby comes, she had better be ready. I even remember telling Meaghan, our wonderful nurse, not to wait to page the doctor because when I say this baby is coming, I literally meant, the baby is coming. She took me seriously and prepped the room for delivery. I knew I liked her. And so like clockwork after breaking my water with the long crochet hook, a fast 45 minutes later, I screamed from the shower.

"I have to push."

And so, I pushed right there; I couldn't move, I was paralyzed by the urge to push. I just stood there with hot water running down on me and pushed. The team started asking me to make my way to the bed and so I did. At this point, I think I was almost buck naked, I didn't care… just as I got back to the bed, I felt the urge to push again. And so I did - standing up. The nurses at this point really wanted me to get into bed and so I wobbled my way up there. I was kneeling at this point, my arms dangling over the top of the bed my face pushed into the pillow.

"I can't do it," I yelled, even this was a little faster than I thought was going to happen. It hurt and I had no painkillers, no epidural. I felt like giving up, except when you are having a baby, there is no quitting, just more pushing.

The nurse got right in my face, just like I asked of her, there was no stroking and telling me how awesome it was, just hardcore, sergeant like commands. She meant business. All I can remember was her yelling in my face was, "Talking isn't pushing, now push!" It was exactly what I needed to hear. I pushed.

And there he was.

Lewiston James Olstad in all his glory, seven pounds and three ounces, born at 8:50am with ten fingers, ten toes, and the softest, sweetest, and most gentle cry ever. They placed him directly on my chest like I asked and I soaked in this healthy little baby boy who was ours. He kept crying, but I didn't mind at all, it was so soft that it just meant he was alive. That soft sweet cry would later haunt us. I couldn't believe we had another babe. Hot Ronnie and I soaked in those precious hours. We smiled at each other not knowing how we were going to do it, but knowing we had each other, and we were building a life together. Lewiston was just meant to be even if he came way sooner than we were ready.

We stayed in the hospital for another eight hours and I asked to get the heck out of there. Hot Ronnie is a major sports fan and his team was in the playoffs. We wanted to get back to our home and so after pushing and prodding the doctors, we got released just hours after I delivered. Lewiston was healthy, feeding well, and we had no concerns. So off we went to take our baby boy to meet our baby girl whose world was about to get rocked.

We now had two babies under thirteen months. Luckily, my mom is the bomb-dot-com and stayed and helped with this crazy transition. Hot Ronnie is always super hands-on; he helps with everything - vacuuming, dusting, the dishes, cooking, and takes care of everything in between. I wish he could stay home with me full-time, but alas, someone has to pay the bills and so he returned to work. I just had a few weeks of being at home by myself during the day before we would take off to Winnipeg for a family vacation, where there would be lots of helping hands.

It was there that Lewiston went floppy; limp, essentially. After a week at a friend's cabin and the most perfect time together, he just had no muscle tone, no strength, no nothing. I took him into emergency after a chiropractor said I needed to do so. She hadn't even treated him - I went to see this chiropractor to help with his colic, but instead, she helped identify his labored breathing, which was something that not even I had noticed.

So off we went to the hospital, but before rushing there, I stopped for a coffee and gluten-free sandwich at my favorite gluten-free bakery, not panicking or worrying - just wanting to be prepared. This was just going to be a routine check and I would rather be safe than sorry. I was convinced that it would take forever to get in as he looked so good. He was healthy, born healthy, he wasn't that limp… or was he? I called my mom on my drive over and asked her to meet me.

Upon our arrival, the first nurse looked at me like I was crazy. As though I was a first-time mom that was super uptight and the kind of mom that freaked out if her kid even sneezed. But after taking his sleeper off and seeing him struggling to breathe, we got taken right back in. I hadn't even had a chance to eat my sandwich yet. What the heck!

After getting ushered right back inside, the next thing I knew, I went from a little curtained off area to the resuscitation room where there were twelve doctors and nurses. They were calling for more specialists and asking if I was okay, they were poking Lewiston, and yelling out his vital statistics… It was like a scene out of a movie.

I remember finally looking around and thinking, *What the F is happening? My son is fine. Why do we need cardiology and neurology? And why is the nurse being so damn nice and holding me up? Why are they asking me if I am okay or if I need to sit and where my husband is, and how fast he could get here?* (Hot Ronnie was back in Calgary, he had left the day before this occurred and drove back my parents' old SUV that they had gifted us, as we only had one car at the time.)

So there I was alone, no Hot Ronnie to comfort me, my mom still en route - feeling utterly puzzled and in total shock at what was happening. The doctors were acting quickly, MRI's were being ordered, and Lewiston's vital signs continued to be tracked. You know when they move fast, something is seriously wrong, because in Canada, if things are not that bad, it takes a long time to get anything done medically. However, when something is wrong, like really wrong, they jump to the pump.

They started asking questions, and I confessed that I had a couple of glasses of wine almost every night at the lake while breastfeeding, and there was the time when his head snapped back really fast while in the carrier and that maybe I paralyzed him... the team assured me this was not the case. The nurse even joked with me saying having two kids under fourteen months deserved a glass of wine or two.

After six exhausting days in the hospital, sleeping on a chair with Hot Ronnie at my feet and Lewiston in my arms, we still had no answers, and they discharged us. We were waiting on a test for Spinal Muscular Atrophy (SMA), you can google it. They said it would take several weeks, they hadn't wanted to test for it, but I demanded it. I was all too familiar with SMA. I had looked after two kids in Calgary with SMA for the last ten years. In fact, three weeks before our holiday to Winnipeg, I went to the bank to get a check for $44,983.00 which I had helped raise for Ishan and Shanaya's wheelchair accessible van.

I was in the room when they drew the blood, I watched them label the vial and I remember asking them to put a rush on the test. Deep in my belly I knew, Lewiston didn't have a virus, but SMA. It just takes a blood test to confirm it. We took a couple of days at my parent's farm to get our feet underneath us. The hospital in Winnipeg had sucked the life out of me and I wanted to get my bearings. Summers in Winnipeg are beautiful; the sunsets are better than anywhere. The sun drops behind the flat prairie fields that my parents have poured their blood, sweat, and tears into for over forty years. My mom and I went out for a walk to watch the sun fall behind their beautiful crop. "It's SMA," I whispered. Tears slowly fell down my face, my bottom lip quivered, and in that moment, I was scared.

"How do you know, why are you so certain?" My mom asked.

"It's his thumb," I replied.

"His thumb?"

"Yes, his thumb. It does the same thing Ishan and Shanaya's thumbs do. I just know it."

Hot Ronnie and I flew back to Calgary the next day. Upon landing, we went to our family doctor who said that this was not the same baby she saw at one week old and sent us straight to Alberta Children's Hospital. It was there we got admitted right away and more testing began. We got our medical records transferred and found out that the hospital staff in Winnipeg never sent off the blood work for SMA testing (they claimed they didn't draw the blood), and we would have to do several of these painful tests over again.

I made our journey public on my Instagram account. It was then that people started following and listening. There was something about Lewiston that could just draw you in. He had these big blue eyes and beautiful long lashes that looked like he had lash extensions. I won't ever have the words to describe just how beautiful he was, but he would capture your attention and all you could see was this beautiful soul that made you want to live better, stand a bit taller, and love that much deeper.

The well-wishes started pouring in - people said stuff like, "We are praying for you," "Don't worry, my daughter had the same thing, and it was just gas..." We prayed for it to be a vitamin deficiency or some bacterial infection that could be treated with antibiotics.

On August 5, 2016, two days before my 32nd birthday, Dr. Jean Mah, the pediatric specialist at Alberta Children's Hospital dropped the bomb that she was certain our son Lewiston had SMA and likely wouldn't make it to his first birthday.

Sorry, what?! SMA, I know it, I look after kids with SMA, they are alive, they are teenagers, they just need wheelchairs, they can't walk, but they made their first birthdays, and then some. Little did I know that type 2 is an entirely different ball game than type 1. Type 1 is the most severe form of SMA, and with how early Lewiston was showing signs, there wasn't much hope. There is no treatment at the time, no cure.

I crumbled, there in that fucking dark room, the blinds were drawn, the machines still beeping and buzzing, that depressing moment - I crumbled. I could barely breathe. Every ounce of hope we had, every belief that we were going to be okay was just robbed from us.

Our son was dying and wouldn't make it to his first birthday. We were just waiting for a blood test to have it confirmed and printed on a piece of paper to make it real. There was no cure, no treatment. It was just a waiting game. In that moment, there was darkness. No light, just utter, cold, and lonely darkness. I am not going to sugarcoat it. A bomb like that could have ripped Hot Ronnie and I apart, but right then and there, after fresh air and having sunshine hit our faces, we made a pact. That no matter what, we were a team. We were going to stick together, have each other's back and that Lewiston's life would be lived joyfully.

And joyful it was.

After getting discharged from that hospital visit, we made it home for several weeks before going back. In September, we got admitted via ambulance when Lewiston was choking and turning blue, and it was then that we never left. We would never take him back home. We would live in that hospital and hospice until his last breath.

Hot Ronnie and I kept our pact and made the moments count. Our community came alongside us in a big way. I even had a group called the "Love For Lewiston Crew" who organized meals, house cleaning, fundraisers, massages, and workouts in the hospice. They kept us going. I can't even count how many friends and family would drop off hot Starbucks. Sometimes over four beverages in a day.

We made his life matter. We documented his every moment and our photographer who did his newborn photos ended up visiting us frequently to capture his life; our life, regardless of how messy it was. I love looking back at the videos and pictures and I always smile seeing his sweet face. I relive those moments, the longing for him deepens but also brings the joy of the time we did have together. Lewiston lived big. We dreamed him up a bucket list and lived it out. He went on a pseudo trip to Vegas with the nurses, he had snowball fights, and felt the first snowflakes of winter, he dressed up as Scuba Steve for Halloween and even proposed to his favorite nurse. On one of our darker days in ICU, a good friend of mine surprised us with Dean Brody, the country singer, and he performed a private concert for us right in Lewiston's room.

We implemented daily dance parties to Justin Timberlake's *Can't Stop the Feeling*, and would have nurses, staff, doctors, and even the head of maintenance join us. It was the best part of each day; it brought smiles to everyone and was a daily ritual that we all looked forward to. Joy was hard to find some days and so we took it upon ourselves to create it. It was a choice, and that is what I believe, kept us upright on the journey.

Those four months in the hospital and hospice were what changed me. Because on August 5, 2016, after my pity party, I was so damn determined to find the light that we didn't have that day. If this had been my diagnosis, I would want to live and live the hell out of life. We fought hard for our son. But we always said, "We fight if he fights, but if he doesn't have fight left, we will let go and let him go."

Our fight was big, we rallied the troops and had offers to fly him to Europe, and for people to lend us their private jets, we got him on a clinical trial which started to make a difference - it was just too late. We did every therapy possible, we prayed, people dropped off crystals for him to sleep on top of, I lathered him in essential oils every day, made him swim, stretch, and do physiotherapy. However, on November 20, 2016, you could tell Lewiston was done fighting and after calling our pastors and dedicating him to the Lord, and of course, praying for one last miracle, we just trusted that the Lord's will be done. Lewiston passed peacefully in my arms on November 22, 2016, after his morning bath. He looked up at my husband and it was as though he said, "Dad, I am going to be alright, but I am done fighting and it is time to let go." He took his last breath and just like that, his earthly body was just a body. Those forty-eight hours of watching our son struggling to breathe and wondering which breath would be his last were the most horrific moments of my life. I pray that no one has to endure that. However, watching my son take his last breath changed me, and it changed others. He started something special which has encouraged us to move, bring joy, and spread love.

In Lewiston losing his life, I have found mine. It is probably the best and the worst thing that has happened to me and us as a couple. It was my slap in the face that I needed to snap out of it and stop coasting. Life changed.

I am now the most alive, most confident, most authentic living Jessica I have ever been. I have always been pretty positive, but in the past, I have struggled with depression and my mental health. I attempted suicide in my second last year of high school and didn't have the courage to own who I was created to be. I was scared to be bold, to be loud, to speak my truths, and talk about what I wanted and dreamed of. I was indeed just humming along. Lewiston's diagnosis changed everything for me, cause all you've got is the days you have and you really never know when they will be taken away.

They say the average person gets 30,000 days, Lewiston's life was nothing close to average and only got 179, but I believe and know that those 179 days were used to touch and change people and the best thing I can do in this world is live out my purpose. I don't know the number of days I have but I do know that I want to live differently. I want joy and boldness. I want to be able to pause and soak in the goodness when it is there, so I am armed to endure the tough stuff. I want to dream and believe that anything is possible.

This is the letter that I wrote to my son on the one year anniversary of his passing. I miss that little blue-eyed angel more than you know. If you are reading this chapter, squeeze your little babes tighter, soak in the moments, and don't wish them away. There is some mama out there that would trade spots with you in a second to have that screaming baby in her arms.

LEWISTON JAMES // To my little babe that danced into heaven way before we were ready for, Thank you for giving me the gift of life. Yes, little man, I am living life with all I got. Truly, you were not planned and came way earlier than we were ready for. I cried when the stick signaled you were on the way. Your sister was only four months old at the time. Little did I know, the short life you would live would be my greatest highlight and most amazing accomplishment. As quickly as you arrived, you were gone. Sometimes the biggest surprises turn out to be the biggest blessings. In losing your life, I have found mine and I believe you are helping others find theirs too. Your dad and I have deepened our marriage and I truly understand what it means to be a loving partner through good times and bad, in sickness and in health. Your handsome dad has kept us together with his unwavering faith and stubbornness. Your big sister is the light we need on tough days and is full of personality. I would have loved to see you two together. Instead, we pray patiently for God to bless us with more brothers and sisters in whichever form they come. We have started a foundation in your honor and memory. I believe your impact is reaching way beyond these Alberta borders. THANK YOU - for showing us that dance brings joy regardless of how dark it is, for spreading love, and helping us choose movement instead of stagnation. We are grateful for all the memories we had. I can't wait to dance in heaven with you, but until then we will live our best life fully alive running right towards our roar.

With all my love, your Mama ~ Jess

~ Heavenly Father - thank you for grace, strength and courage. Your love is enough. To Jodie and Kristin, thank you for creating space and loving me. This chapter would not have come together without you. To my girls crew, my family, Miss Swayzie Grace and Lewiston James - without you none of this is possible. And finally to the hottest hubby, Hot Ronnie, your support is unwavering and your love never ending, there aren't enough words. I love you, and am thankful.

Section 3

CULTIVATING YOUR VILLAGE WHILE DESIGNING THE FUTURE

FEATURING
Jordan Paige
Stephanie Fox
Caitlyn Laird
Janice Meredith
Neli Tavares Hession

OPENING COMMENTARY BY
Sabrina Greer

I REMEMBER WHEN I FIRST STARTED MODELING (a career that spanned over two decades for me), I got a job for a prominent magazine. I was so excited. *This was it, my big break.* I showed up for work on the coldest day of the year and was handed a rack of bathing suits and told to get in the pond, *the unheated, outdoor, murky pond.* They had to paint my skin to make it "less blue" and I had to fake smile through chattering teeth. I recall thinking to myself, *This isn't glamorous at all, this is* hard. I also remember my first big gig as an event director, ten years later. Three thousand guests, sixty-five staff, all reporting to me. I was the boss and very proud of what I had pulled together so flawlessly. At 3am, as I was on my hands and knees scraping cigarette butts and bubble gum off the concrete and sorting through garbage, I also recall thinking, *This is pretty tough too.* University exams, *difficult.* Closing the bar late nights, getting hit on by the last man standing while counting inventory, *also challenging.*

I've had a lot of jobs in my life, and almost all of them at some point were tough. Not one of them, however, compares to motherhood. I'm not just talking about the day-to-day grind of being a full-time chef, housekeeper, chauffeur, teacher, and overall superhero, which is obviously challenging and exhausting. I'm talking about the responsibility we have to raise these little people into proper ladies and gentlemen. The pressure to provide them the tools they need to thrive in this crazy world, now that's hard.

This section, much like the other sections in this book had a theme too. Community! We've all heard the saying, "*It takes a village to raise a child,*" right? I wanted to better understand this concept as it kept coming up throughout the writing process. I delved deeper into my research. I interviewed a dozen moms (in addition to the amazing authors in this book) and asked what the concept of "village" meant to them in reference to their children. What did they do when things got "hard," who did they speak to?

Most mothers felt as though they had no village. One mom with two children (three-years-old, and almost two) had never been away from her boys for more than six hours (*no more than six hours in three years, excuse me!*). Another mother said she spends ninety-eight percent of her time alone with her children at home, she has diapers and groceries delivered to the door and most of her friends do not have children, making socializing challenging. *How insanely isolating*, I thought. This aided in the discovery of what I am calling the **supermom phenomenon**. We, as moms, feel like we must do it all and put unrealistic expectations on ourselves to not just do it all, but do it all well, all the time, all alone. It seems it is not uncommon for mothers to operate a home-based business or multiple businesses while caring solo for their children, and the home at the same time. While it is very inspiring to watch someone multitask on this level, I'm certain it is a sure way to burn out fast.

When I think of the word village, I think of a sisterhood, a club of like-minded individuals that love and support each other unconditionally. Motherhood, in my opinion, is not something you should do without backup. I'm not suggesting that you **can't** do it all, I'm merely encouraging you not to. All moms need support. Remember this is the most challenging JOB you will ever have. Imagine for a moment: You are hired by a corporation, and do not receive a training manual and to boot have no support. You are just given the job and expected to figure it out, sound familiar? We all need a judgment-free place where, at the very least, we can discuss just being a mom, bounce some ideas around, and get some help. Let's be honest folks, red-cape or not, mommin' ain't easy!

The current dictionary definition of a "village" is a "self-contained district or community within a designated area." However, the concept has existed for decades and means so much more. "It takes a village" is an African proverb from the 50s according to *Random House Dictionary of American Proverbs and Sayings*,"Omwana ni wa bhone," in Kijita translates to *"Regardless of a child's biological parent(s), its upbringing belongs to the community."* I lived by this quote, quite literally for most of my life. I not only have three adopted siblings but grew up with dozens of foster siblings. I never batted an eye. My parents were foster parents, and that was just the way it was.

It was modeled for me from a very young age that it is okay to **ask for help** and that parenting is not something you do solely with one partner. We had a revolving door of social workers, occupational therapists, community helpers, teachers, mentors and friends, my grandfather lived with us in a separate apartment, and we called my parents' friends - aunts and uncles. This translated over into my teenage years when my home became a place of refuge for friends in need. This learned skill set of acceptance and flexibility has served me well in motherhood. It is ok to request support. You are a warrior anyway and do not need to prove to anyone that you can do "it all." What you need to do is drop "it all" and go have some fun!

In her book, *The Village Effect*, psychologist Susan Pinker explains that humans are hard-wired to connect with other human beings. She goes as far to say, "There is no substitute for human interactions and that this is a matter of life and death, neglecting to keep in close contact with people who are important to you is **at least** as dangerous to your health as a pack-a-day cigarette habit, hypertension or obesity." As we embark on this new digital generation, a place where we can avoid human contact if desired, I think it is important to remember this. So go have brunch with your childless girlfriends while daddy watches the monsters. Go dancing, participate in group fitness classes, or find a social hobby. Join mom-and-baby groups that involve human interaction. Get outside, breathe fresh air, move your body, and engage in human contact. Normalize human connection again. Show your children what it means to be part of a community, how to develop relationships with real people, not screens (at least some of the time). **Your children are always paying attention, teach them how to build their village by going out and building yours.**

11

BE NOT THE ARCHITECT, BUT THE INSPIRATION

by Jordan Paige

"We do not get to be the architect of their entire lives."

Jordan Paige

Growing up a highly sensitive, emotionally intuitive, and creative child, Jordan has always been drawn to the arts. Her irreverent humor, inherent people pleasing, yet headstrong personality helped her navigate two large moves during childhood. Landing in Calgary when she was eleven years old, Jordan found herself a fish out of water. Excelling in dance from age four, training and becoming a Canadian champion baton twirler helped her find her physical and artistic outlets as well as a community of like-minded kids which built her confidence.

Jordan left home at seventeen for modelling and dance contracts that took her around the globe for the rest of her teens and the majority of her twenties. Through modelling, she found herself booking and enjoying shooting commercials worldwide which led to a successful acting career that carried into her thirties. Though modelling and acting gives her a rewarding and adventurous life, she has always had secret dreams of telling her own stories. Jordan has recently finished multiple children's books based on adoption and non traditional families, and is working on her first screenplay.

Being intensely empathetic has served Jordan well in her acting career. Writing from a place of sensitivity and understanding of both her own and others' fears and passions. Jordan tells stories in a hilarious, yet meaningful and emotional tone stemming from a wide breadth of life experience. Jordan lives in Toronto with her husband Johnny, and their two boys.

Also, she swears a lot.

ig: @jpmadley | @jmadwunder

"Children are not things to be molded,
but are people to be unfolded."
~ Jess Lair

I TRUSTED IN THE UNIVERSE. I trusted that my little one would come when they were ready. A year full of tears and disappointments, supplements, artificial inseminations, heartache, and hope. When he finally came, I felt bonded immediately. Without knowing if I was pregnant with a boy or a girl, I somehow knew exactly who this little one was. What their passions would be, their struggles and strengths, that their little disposition would perfectly complement my own. I could see us walking hand in hand a few years later, through the farmer's market picking out our produce for yet another perfect homemade meal. A peaceful storybook home life, our consummate calm oasis. I prayed, chanted, and ate all organic. I played music for my baby and rubbed my homemade essential oil-infused lotion on my belly every day. I took care of us. We were us now, and I would make life perfect. From the time I was old enough to understand family structure, I had known that motherhood was my path. I would have a beautiful wedding, five children, everything would be made from scratch, and would never lose my patience. I would be the architect of the perfect family, bestowing the perfect childhood upon my children and I was honored that it was time.

My pregnancy was blissful. I felt empowered and goddess-like, not a moment of sickness or second-guessing my abilities. *I got this. I know what this looks like. No one is more ready.* I hypno-birthed, I meditated, and I practiced the Bradley Method. All in preparation for a joyous natural birthing experience that would connect me with all women who came before, birthing in caves on fur by fire. It was an honor to be trusted with this life, and I refused to numb but a moment of the experience.

My water broke, and I did not go into labor. I was induced, I did not progress, and I needed an epidural. After my son was born, I was bleeding profusely, and my child was not breathing. There was no gentle dancing to soft music or meditating my way through contractions. There was fear, trauma, the pediatric emergency team and the Neonatal Intensive Care Unit (NICU). *How could I possibly have felt so entitled to a perfect experience? How did I not plan for this? I should've written a will. I should have made arrangements in case I didn't make it through this.* My son was finally placed on my belly. In the most profound moment in all my life, I thought... so, THIS *is love. Also, I have no idea who the hell this is.*

Only in recent years have we seemed to truly grasp, or be open to the concept that our children are not blank slates. My sheer arrogance in feeling I knew exactly who this person was, hit me the moment his naked little wrinkly self was placed upon me. Children, unbeknownst to me at the time, are not a mathematical equation; the sum of our DNA, divided by two, equaling the perfect mix of who we think we are in our best moments. That's not to say I didn't feel connected. I felt utterly and intrinsically attached, and for the first time in my life, unconditional love. I was just blindsided by the realization that he was not mine. He was OF ME; but he was not my belonging. I had no right to say or assume who he was. He was made of love, cells, stardust, and born through all my positive intentions. He was not property on whom I could impose... a damn thing, really. I remember looking at my little one and silently vowing to let him reveal himself to me in his own way, in his own time. Soon after he was born, I was left a single mom, no help, no money, and no childcare. Along with the blueprint for my life going up in flames went the safety in thinking I could control the outcome of anything. Some of the best advice I was ever given in my life was to always be the student. To not be afraid of not knowing, to have the courage to ask questions. Having all my perfect plans erupt Mount Vesuvius style left me no choice but to be that student. So I would be, of parenthood, of my child. I would be open to where life would take us. They say loss of control can be freeing, but seriously, at this juncture, it was some crazy scary shit.

I will humbly hump the leg of any single parent in true admiration, including myself. Which is good, because self-humping is something you need to get down with if you're a single parent of a new baby. Though I digress. I'm sure you all feel this way at times; single, married, older, younger - parenthood will take you to exactly one hair shy of what you think you are capable of. Every spiritual, physical, and emotional limit pushed to the brink. When you think you don't have it in you to lift them one more time, you do. When you can't stay awake for one more minute, you do. And when you couldn't possibly love them more than at that very moment, do you ever. You know that stage, it's brief but feels everlasting, when they're teething, and if you so much as move one hand off them to change the channel they lose their minds? That stage where they must be held and rocked while standing and shifting your weight for hours on end, and GODDAMN YOU if you think for one second you can sneak a snack and place them down! Your arms, back, and soul are all weary. Putting your cell phone in the fridge, and having eye cream on your toothbrush is totally normal because, ya know, a brain can only thrive on trail mix and a cracker for so long. I don't know how I made it through that. I peed my pants. That's not some cute idiom for how I felt in the moment. I peed my pants. I remember spending half a dozen hours with a dreary-eyed little teething angel in my arms who just couldn't sleep. He was so precious, he was so exhausted, and in such pain. When he finally dozed off in my arms, being gently swayed from side to side, I was dying to use the loo. I knew that if I so much as moved two steps, he would be up. I consciously decided to stand on a towel, let the air out of the balloon, so to speak, and stay there until he was asleep enough for me to put down. That may not be the only time or context in which I have soiled myself, but that is another book and *none of yer goddamned business.*

I remember someone telling me (a year too late of course), that instead of reading book after book about labor and delivery while pregnant, one should read actual parenting books. Labour is one day, ish. Baby then comes home. Baby then lives with you... for a long time. Once baby arrives, there is no time for perusing texts on why your nipples go zing! Like you stuck your finger in a socket when your let-down kicks in. There are few to absolutely zero minutes to research that menacing wet spot that keeps appearing on baby after a diaper change, forcing you to change his entire outfit again. P.S. It's your right teet leaking through your shirt because you forgot to reinsert that breast pad. You're welcome. There will be 1,476,003 questions you will have. Most of which Google has 1,476,003 answers for. We have doctors, pediatricians, midwives, blogs, and Facebook groups we can quite easily reach out to for most of our queries regarding health, logistics, basic rants, and what to do when your little one shits in the shower (BTW, it depends on the consistency). I also had great people in my life who offered me their support. People, I will never quite know how to thank, without whom I would've drowned. I had lifelines, and their kindness will forever bring me to my knees. Family and friends who gave us a roof over our heads, food to eat, loving support in ways big and small. My people showed up, and not the expected people. Unanticipated acts of kindness quite literally saved us.

That being said, I was a single mom, and have never felt more alone, and scared. I also felt, at times, incredible and harsh judgment with a hefty dose of pity. Everyone offered advice on how to fix my life: To be vengeful, move on quickly, make lots of money, and approach the legalities like war. There was a lot of pressure to figure it all out quickly in a way that made my situation feel palatable to others. Every waking moment, I immersed myself in being the best parent I could be, and I didn't have the bandwidth or the capability to consider the broader and more long-term issues. The all-encompassing, solitary, job, and honor of parenthood was in session. This little man depended on me now, and I would be his rock, always. I would make damn sure that he would look back on his childhood and not feel a lack of anything, especially love. I felt that I had to make up for so much and overshoot the mark on every front. Also, on some level, I knew I didn't have the answers, and so I was terrified of asking myself the questions; to look down the road and envision how things would unfold. Too many variables, too much pain to face. The path to peace would have to wait.

Between full-time single parenthood and one's own resentment and hurt, it is so easy to remain lost in feeling lost. My heart broke for my son. Had I the energy or the luxury of time for self-pity, my heart would've broken for me as well. It's so difficult to articulate your heart space at this time. Isn't it, single, separated, and divorced parents? On the one hand, there is such fear and turmoil, and on the other, this gorgeous mountain of love which keeps you floating through your days and knowing, somehow, it will all be okay. You'll do whatever it takes to make it okay. You'll make it amazing.

So here you are. You are divorced, or you are separated, or you are single. The need to walk through the legal shit storm lands at your door in the way of custody papers. In my case, the other parent had been absent for almost a year. I reached out, got approved for legal aid, set up a free mediator, and hoped for the best. I needed to get my boy into subsidized daycare, so I could get back to work and provide for us. Days after mediation, I was texted, "I will never give you sole custody. I am not signing these papers." Then boom, custody papers appeared. For the record, I would've done the same. Minus the significant time periods of absence, of course. The ability to put off all the long-term questions and appropriate solutions evaporates. You have no choice but to face it as fear, and fury floods your very being. This felt so much worse than being alone. It felt like war. No holds barred, personal, gloves off, face punching, gut-wrenching awfulness. I made the decision immediately that I was not going to lose who I was in this process. I had heard such awful stories of this time in the lives of others. Remaining true to the woman and mother I was, I would walk through this with an open heart, and be someone my son would be proud of. I was going to maintain my integrity, advocate for what was best for my child, and let the chips fall where they may, instead of perpetuating a war based solely on what I wanted, or felt I was entitled to. Most importantly, I was never going to act out of spite. Now let's be clear, I wanted to. I wanted this person to know he deserved nothing from us. Not our time, our understanding, not my kindness, or conciliatory efforts. But for whatever reason, my higher self kicked in, and I looked at my child and chose peace. I knew the two of us as parents could not teach him about lifelong commitment, but we had every opportunity to use our situation to show him the value of respect, kindness, forgiveness, and grace in the face of adversity. I envisioned backyard barbecues with new partners, all our children playing in the yard as we cracked open a beer and laughed. We were friends before we were more, couldn't we just be that again? For that, you need two willing participants. What it takes to sail into your higher self, a place where you can genuinely desire a friendship, or even just an amicable rapport, after all the trust, love, and safety has been lost, is profound. The personal work, the inner healing, the letting go that is required, is work which will benefit your life, mental health, and happiness regardless of what you are met with on the other side. In doing that work, I found my path to peace. A place where I have never been happier or more settled. I have never trusted more or been more open to love. I am happy. I am free. I am the best mama I can be because of it.

THE PATH TO PEACE

Take a deep breath, have a glass of wine or scotch. Have a bath and get into your happy place. Do some meditating and raise your vibration, Mama. This is an earnest and honest attempt to find your path to peace.

Is Your Child Safe In Their Care?

I won the single mom lottery. I have the most incredible husband. He is honest, and he is kind. He is funny as hell and is emotionally communicative. He is the most natural parent I have ever known. He never puts the toothpaste away. He has his iPhone at the dinner table. He cuts our boys' apples in a way that makes no sense to me and still leaves half the f*cking core still inside! My point is this; they will never do it all up to your standards, and that's okay. Your ex will undoubtedly do things differently and there is a learning curve that deserves some patience, especially if they're showing up a little late on game day. It is so easy, and for a moment feels so vindicating, to blast them when they do something wrong, or different. You'll think, *That's not what he's used to!* or, *You're doing it wrong!* And it's not, and they may be. Just ask yourself if your child is safe, truly safe, in their care. Even if you are in a partnership with someone raising children, you will still get stressed over how you deal differently with your kids. Hopefully, the basics of child-rearing, fundamental philosophies are in alignment, but not always! Consider giving your child's parent the same space to find their parenting groove you would give to a current partner. Free from overly harsh judgment, no matter how much you may be dying to make them feel stupid or incapable. It does not serve you, nor does it serve your child. At some point, if not now, your child will be alone in their care, and they deserve to feel safe. So if you believe they are safe in the other parent's care, let them feel it. Find security in reminding yourself of that fact.

Does Love Lead?

Kids are all too often used as weapons, and we know this. A good friend of mine, an inspirational and empowering mother who is a beacon of love and light, separated from her little one's father before her son was born. The father insisted on overnights from the time the little one was a few months old, and still exclusively breastfeeding. Most of you will gasp at this alone. The most unsettling part was that he would then get a babysitter and go out at night. It became clear that the overnight was more about taking the little one from the mother than actually having bonding and nurturing parenting time with the infant. That does not, by the way, mean he doesn't love his son. I just think it raises red flags. It puts into question if the parent is capable of putting the child's best interests ahead of their own bitterness or feelings of entitlement. You will undoubtedly disagree about frequency and readiness for overnights, holidays, yadda yadda yadda… But ask yourself this, does love lead?

Can You Agree On Mutual Non-Disparagement?

Since the beginning of my solo mama journey, I have sought the advice of friends, early childhood psychologists, divorced parents, and adults who were children from nontraditional families. One conversation has stuck in my mind for a few years now. A colleague of mine said she always resented her mother for speaking negatively about her dad. He was not a great father and never around, but what stayed with her into adulthood was how much stress hearing all that negativity caused her. Whether it was just little jabs, comments the mother thought she may not even understand yet, or big emotional and verbal upheavals - it caused anxiety that lasted a lifetime. It is commonly known now that children that come from homes where parents disparage one another have issues with self-esteem.[4] Again, we still have every opportunity to teach kids positive traits and empowering emotions which help build their own value and self-worth through these unintended circumstances.

....

4 Sedacca, R. (2012, April 18). "Post-Divorce Parenting: Bashing Your Ex Is Bad for Your Children." *The Huffington Post*, Retrieved from www.huffingtonpost.com/rosalind -sedacca/post-divorce-parenting_b_1421494.html.

Consider a frank, if brief conversation, with your ex, talking about the benefits of positively addressing and referring to each other to and around your kids. I know, you're not there yet, but one day... Once in a blue moon, pick something your ex is great at and highlight it to your kid. It'll feel good, I promise. Or it won't. But one day, they'll look back and get to know that you never played dirty. That you selflessly did everything in your power to promote a positive and healthy relationship between parent and child. It'll feel good then.

Support Love From All Sources

As an adopted child, I deeply understand the need to connect to our heritage, our ancestry, our people. The answers to our most rudimentary questions, "Who are we?" and "Where do we come from?" is something no child should be denied. I don't pretend to know all of your situations, but I do know that the desire to cut out a parent who has wronged you, and sometimes in doing so... wronged your child, can be strong. But I firmly believe all children, when appropriate, safe, loving, and possible, deserve every chance to thrive in relationships that bring them love and connect them to where they come from. We do not own them; we do not get to be the architect of their entire lives. Our kids deserve all the love this world has to offer even if it comes from a source you're not crazy about. Let love in, for them. I always think that if ever something were to happen to me, I want my child to have people. To have a thriving community and loads of family who makes them feel safe and loved.

Happy people make better parents. Accepting an ex's new partner can be tough. I always wanted mine to find someone wonderful pretty quick. It made me feel better knowing there would be a woman, who hopefully had some maternal instinct, in the house to help care for my child. I want my little guy to be in a loving family setting when he has to spend nights away someday. Consider the emotional and logistical surroundings you wish for your little people when you're not there. We must find it within ourselves to support the other parent's happiness and new families. Those are our children's step and half-siblings, they're family as well. Let them give and receive all the love they possibly can, and let them never feel guilty about it. It's funny, I once dated a divorced man with a son. He never had a nice word to say about his ex-wife. Well through co-parenting with this woman, whom I was fully expected to despise, I fell in love with her. She is brilliant, loving, is generous of heart, and an inspirational single mom. Unbeknownst to me at the time, I learned invaluable lessons for my future from her. The guy turned out to be a turd wrapped in mold fermenting in the hot sun, but half a decade later, she is still one of my best friends! The moral of that story: Be open to love. For yourself and your child, encourage and support love from every person possible.

Teach Your Child Emotional Literacy

I can imagine you, like me, worry a great deal about all the disappointments your child could face in their young life. Helping them navigate through their tender years in a nontraditional family and how it will affect the adult they will become is crucial. Raising them is the most important work we'll ever do, and this is one of the most challenging aspects of that. How do we shield them from hurt and disappointments? We can't. What we can do is to teach them to greet each day as though the sun is going to brightly shine through their window. And when the rain comes in, be there to gently dry their cheeks. Give them the words to express their emotions. Big words, specific words. Let them know the difference between sad and disappointed, hurt and angry. Let them use those words and hold space for their big feelings. Try your best not to take any of it personally if it's directed at you, and don't rush to fix it. Let them feel what they feel and support their expression of it. That goes for the happy stuff too! "Oh you and papa made Legos today, and you had so much fun? That's awesome! That makes mama so happy!" It's scary how smart these little guys are. They know to people please from a very young age - they know what we want and don't want to hear. If they feel bad expressing the good stuff they want to share, there is less of a chance they'll express themselves when they feel yucky feelings. I make sure my little one is excited to share his joys with me and feels safe expressing his sorrows. He tells me everything, quite literally, everything! So as worried as you will remain about all that could go wrong, just make sure you set yourselves up with stellar communication skills.

Okay, how's that wine? That wasn't so bad, huh? So if you're able to answer those questions and take those steps, then it's time for the final one...

Let Go and Let God, Broad!

A perfect childhood does not make a perfect child. If it's Jesus, Buddha, Allah, Mother Earth, your long-departed Nana, or the dog you buried in the backyard - CALL IT IN, SISTER! Hold whatever you believe in within your heart and trust, TRUST that the Universe is giving your child (and YOU) the adversity, the karma, the experiences, and the lessons to help them become the best person they can be! This is THEIR life. We can not write every scene, and there is truthfully so little we can control. Honor their journey and all that the world brings to them. It's not about it being perfect; it's about our perspective and how we deal with what comes our way. Take all that bitterness, resentment, and negativity and toss it like a fart in the wind! (Thanks to my dad for that expression). We create our children's emotional environment. Let yours be one of positivity, love, and peace. This may be the actual moment I fell in love with my husband. Close to the beginning of our relationship, in a conversation regarding my relationship with the ex, he said, "Be open to the possibility that it could be amazing!" Ladies, be open to the possibility that it could be amazing! It may feel like walking through fire to get to that place. It's going to be uncomfortable at times. But we love these little creatures. And sometimes, love means peeing your pants for someone!

~ This piece is dedicated to my glorious community. Especially the McKean and Forbes-Lawrence families, who gave us a safe haven when we had nowhere to turn. To my friend, Steven Mann, who always gives this "fatty" the straight skinny, who always has my back and will never let me fall. This is for my Johnny, who truly sees me for everything I am and everything I am not, and honors and loves me because, and in spite of it all! To my beautiful baby soulmates, my boys; choosing me to be your mama is the greatest gift on earth. You are everything. I will grow, and fight to be worthy of you every day of my life.

12

IT TAKES A VILLAGE, NOW BUILD YOURS, UNAPOLOGETICALLY

by Stephanie Fox

"The sacrifices you make are what allow for the possibilities in your life."

Stephanie Fox

Vice President | Mother of Two
Water and Mountains Addict | Cookbook Collector

Stephanie has built a successful career as a leader in the nonprofit sector. Driven by her compassion for others, she entered the philanthropic world, raising money for those in need. Through her leadership and strategic direction, she has increased capacity across community, higher education, and healthcare organizations to affect positive change in the lives of others. In her own development, she has learned alongside colleagues in the United States, Europe and Asia. The middle child between two brothers, she quickly developed a competitive and persevering spirit, a constant craving for adventure, the confidence to hold her own in any environment, and learned to view obstacles simply as something to get over, around, or through. Whether in the boardroom, downhill skiing, galloping on horseback, or wearing her children's favorite hedgehog print apron in the kitchen, Stephanie is in her element. Truly an old-soul, her warmth, caring demeanor, unwavering loyalty, and selfless nature are qualities remarked upon and treasured by many. Her "you've got this" approach has propelled others around her to realize their own potential. Of her many loves and experiences, her greatest joy (and challenge) has been becoming a mother to her two incredible daughters, Leah and Claire. She credits them for the joy, learning, and motivation that fills each day and looks forward to all that the three of them will experience tomorrow.

ig: @redfoxski

"Individually, we are one drop. Together, we are an ocean."
~ Ryunosuke Satoro

IT WAS A THURSDAY EVENING, and I was across the ocean (again) for an annual conference in Dublin, Ireland. My red hair has always made me feel at home "across the pond," however, now in my thirties and as a mother of two young daughters, I'm always thinking about my real home, no matter how many time zones widen the distance between us.

Here on another conference, I enjoyed an exhilarating day of learning and sharing with colleagues from around the world, our day ending with the conference staple; a networking reception where the greatest amount of sharing and learning happen, and ultimately, where inspiration is found. I stood in an above-street venue in bustling Temple Bar, immersed in conversations with other women leading the charge in the nonprofit sector through working for organizations that are saving and changing lives. We not only discussed the headway we were making in our respective roles, but also shared details of our lives at home. We celebrated the change we were affecting, the differences made in the lives of others, the copious amount of work left to be done, and ultimately, how we compensated for the missed time at home to make it all happen. Some details of our shared experience at home were joyous, while others were torturous. No matter, we were all finding comfort in many of the same things and being challenged, at times seemingly beaten, by other parts of home life. It was yet another moment in my professional life where I was, without a doubt, exactly where I was meant to be.

I specify "professional life" because it is one very significant part of my life, but it doesn't represent all of it. As mothers, compartmentalization becomes not only a habit for some, but ostensibly a prerequisite to succeeding in any one area. In certain stages of one's career, pressure may exist to have children be seemingly non-existent to be viewed as being dedicated, focused, and reliable. I recall my colleague being shocked upon finding out I had children... after a year of working beside one another. Similarly, in "mom-life," the pressure is no less. There are intrinsic and extrinsic forces that lead to how we describe ourselves; while I, at one time, referred to myself as a "career-focused mother of two," the descriptive has evolved to, "career-loving." This is not only more palatable for both audiences of career and motherhood, but also for myself. Who exactly is ever singularly focused? I can't recall the last time I had the luxury of being singularly focused on anything. Can you?

But it's not that simple. I wish it were, but there's always more to the story, and here it is; one of the things I value most about my friendships is how eclectic my group of friends are and the diverse experience and perspectives they offer. Still, I'd be lying if I said judgment didn't exist on occasion when I beamed about something work-related. The unasked question was, "Why is she not beaming about her children?" One can be ecstatic when talking about one's children and also be the same when sharing a career-related moment. There has always been pressure to be viewed as loving parts of life at appropriate levels, but how often do we really take stock of everything in our life that falls into this bucket? We are women, partners, mothers, professionals, and friends. We often set immense and unmovable expectations of ourselves to deliver in all areas. But, we can't be in multiple places at once nor can we simultaneously split our time equally between the people who fill our lives.

While I was at the conference, my two daughters, ages four and five (I know, it's only now starting to make sense as to why I had them fifteen months apart), were at home in Atlantic Canada with their grandparents. It was 11:21pm (UK time) when my personal phone (and yes, my work phone has its own distinct set of signals) buzzed the unique vibration that says, "This isn't a text, or an irrelevant social media update but an email from your home-life." Politely excusing myself from the conversation, I made my way through the crowd and away from the energy that Dublin naturally offers, and touched on the notification; an email from my father appeared with the subject line: "Leah lost her wheels." Within that email was a partial photo of my oldest daughter on her bicycle, cruising down the lake road at our cottage. My heart sank. I held my breath and, with great hesitancy, opened the email and attached photo. There, the star of the picture was a five-year-old girl, her blonde ponytail lifting off her back in the artificial wind created by her acceleration, a smile so wide, one would ask if it was possible to be any happier than she was in that moment. It was a point in time that exemplified perfect joy, accomplishment, and absolute pride. It was in equal parts for me in that moment, a celebratory milestone, and a cringe-worthy realization. I wasn't there.

I quickly scrambled for a point of reference. My mind flashed back to the day I "lost my wheels." My father, home from work, had followed up on the notice he had given the week before that it would be this evening that I would lose my training wheels; countless tries of me pedaling, with my father running alongside me, while I shouted, "I'm not ready. Don't let go!" But on the final try, my father did let go. For a few moments, the space between his hand, and the handle of my banana seat bike, distanced. I felt the rush of independently passing my driveway and approaching the neighbor's house, and then going over the handlebars, my face meeting the pavement before any part of my body and having a bloody mess to show for it. But my father was there to pick me up. My mother was there to hug me and tend to my wounds when I entered the house, a sobbing mess of blood and tears. On a Dublin sidewalk, I was not there for Leah. There have been an equal amount of times that I have not been present for Claire.

As mothers tend to do, my mind then rushed to all the other points in time I was unable to be "there." I recalled the "Kick-Off to Kindergarten" meeting earlier that spring, for which I was absent and had asked another parent for notes upon my return. Fast forward to the next month's kindergarten orientation, I, fully aware that I would miss it, had covered my absence by enlisting my mother to take my daughter to school and a neighbor-friend to accompany her on the bus for the trial run. As I sat in meetings in Toronto, I knew my child would be the only one without a parent by their side that day. Apart from getting updates from my mother and neighbor, a most welcome call came from one of my colleagues. It was between meetings in the back of a Toronto cab that my work cell buzzed with an incoming call from Eileen. I answered, anticipating a work conversation. Instead, I was met with, "Guess who Anna's reading buddy is?!" In that question, my world opened up. I had an inside line to my daughter's day. Eileen's daughter in senior year had been matched with my daughter as a mentor to kindergarten. My excitement matched that in Eileen's voice while hearing the story of Leah and Anna's day together.

My mind was brought back to the present moment: Standing alone on a Dublin sidewalk, staring at a photo of my daughter biking independently down a country road. And it was in this moment, where my perspective shifted, altering how I viewed the balance of my contributions to, and time away from, my children.

As a (happily divorced) single parent, I have been primarily responsible for my daughters from the time they were both under eighteen months. Despite being outnumbered and single-handed, I had advanced my career beyond the level met by many two-parent, double-income households around me (a topic for a separate book!). To say this has not been without sacrifice would be an understatement.

Monitoring where we spend our time and deciding who and what gets which parts of us is a conversation many of us have with ourselves on a (I argue overly) frequent basis. It also causes us to constantly ask ourselves the questions (among others), "Are my priorities the right ones?" and "Should I change how much time I'm giving to them (competing priorities)?" There was a time when I evaluated every hour past the forty hour work week mark against the time I was missing with my children. *Was this gala dinner, evening board meeting, or the like, really worth it? Am I having dinner with my CEO more than I am my family?*

Work-life balance does not exist as a constant state of being. It is a concept. The idea that it's possible for one to prioritize the demands of career and personal life on a continual basis so that all resources (time and otherwise) are perfectly allocated at all times, is (brace yourself), unrealistic.

Among the definitions provided by Oxford Dictionaries, balance is defined as:

- An even distribution of weight enabling someone or something to remain upright and steady.
- A situation in which different elements are equal or in the correct proportions.
- Compare debits and credits in (an account) to ensure they are equal.

When contextualizing these definitions into our lives, what comes to mind? How does it make you feel? For many of us, comparing our work-life prioritization against the definition of balance could elicit either laughter or tears. When reflecting on points in my own life relative to such definitions, there were times when I felt as though I would figuratively fall on my face (or literally, due to exhaustion… seriously, I started drinking coffee post first baby as a survival tactic), which hardly seemed "equal or in the correct proportions," and regardless of who or what was receiving my time and energy, the debits grossly outweighed the credits.

So why exactly, is this constant state of work-life balance, which so many of us aspire to, not realistically achievable and why is it important for us to be accepting of this reality? While it's important to evaluate how we strive to "balance" work and personal life, we must first acknowledge the following: A constant state of work-life balance is made impossible due to the ever-present reality of work-life conflict. Every moment I'm in the office, I recognize this is time missed with Leah and Claire. Likewise, every moment I'm at home, I'm acutely aware that work is piling up. Our time cannot be simultaneously divided across competing priorities… trust me, I've tried. To be present and excelling in one area, we cannot be present in another area. Sometimes, my CEO and organization will get my time. Other times, my children will own it. There is always a sacrifice to something. So to excel in one area, how do we best compensate in another? By 1) Building the most incredibly supportive, connected, village we can, and 2) Organizing how we interweave ourselves between our work and own home-made village. While I'll be referring to the first point in the context of family, having a strong village in one's work life is also vital. I'm certain I'm reaching the eye-roll stage with my work team over my frequent exclamation, *"Team work makes the dream work!"*

Building The Strongest Village

As with any structure, it's only as strong as its foundation. The foundation for your life's most valued parts is you, and **only** you. If you were to build a house, no amount of lumber, nails, siding, or shingles could make up for a weak foundation. In the case of your supporting village, they can't replace you. Truly. Is this a terrifying analogy? Yes. But you can do it. You're stronger than perhaps you know or even realize.

Over the holiday season, I took a weekend flight a few provinces away to attend a function at a friend's home. What began initially as polite small talk with another guest I had just met, soon evolved into a very real, unfiltered discussion on parenting and specifically, the help we need but won't allow ourselves to accept. As he asked about my "village" at home, he seemed both excited about the structure of support I had built around me, but at the same time, visibly saddened. I asked what kept his family busy and if he and his wife had extended family or others to help. With a grimace, he quietly replied, "We had a nanny once, but it didn't work out." Not wanting to be intrusive, I glazed over his response by stating, "Yes, it's not always easy to find the right fit." What he said next was what so many of us feel internally when we must invite help into our family, but in my years of being a mother, have never heard it said aloud, "My wife was scared our daughter would love the nanny more than her."

It cannot be overstated how incredibly important you are, and always will be, to those around you even in the times you're not physically present. I have yet to return home from a business trip where I'm not greeted at the door with shrieks of joy from two beautiful, blonde-haired wonders lunging at me for the first hug. While all their needs are met and they feel loved by others while I am away, there is no replacement. Your love, intention, and unwavering dedication are what is needed when inviting members of your "village" to build the strongest, weather-resistant, crisis overcoming, screw you Hurricane (insert most present challenge here), home you can imagine.

What are the needs of your home? What does the perfect village look like to support your needs? This question must be truthfully, and unapologetically, answered by you. Of all the compartments that we create for ourselves and others (while they need to be considered in your life), the only answers that are truly representative of your needs can be settled on by you. For some of us, the question might be, "What help do I need on Mondays?" While for others, the question may be, "What help do I need every day throughout the year?"

It wasn't on a sidewalk in Dublin that I began building my village. It is there that I accepted my village unapologetically and celebrated it. So how do we trade in guilt for acceptance? We do so by clearly understanding what outcome we want to create. This then leads to acceptance. By accepting the support needed to allow us to meet our goals and desired outcomes, and celebrating what is possible and can stop seeing sacrifices as an action to feel guilty about. And instead, be proud of the possibilities we create in our lives because we were willing to make those sacrifices.

Affording my children a life full of experiences I wish to provide, has meant advancing my career over and above what would ever be possible on my own. While in our hearts, we always want to be close to our children, in practicality, we must accept welcoming others into our lives who support us to be our best in the many parts that make us whole. In the absence of challenge and sacrifice, we cannot grow for ourselves or those around us.

Gratitude - Celebrating Your Village

"I don't know how you do it," a most common observation from colleagues and new friends. "I don't," is my standard response. There are so many members of my village who I credit for the role they play in the wonderful details that fill my family's life. My constant and public expressions of gratitude for all that they offer aren't just with the intention of making them feel valued. The other equally important outcome is that everyone else around me knows how significant they are in my life. By doing so, I am signaling to all that not only do I unapologetically rely on my village, but I celebrate the gifts of their time, and welcome their love into my home and for my children. To keep them organized quietly behind the scenes would send a very different message; it would imply that I feel I should be doing it all on my own and that I'm flawed or deficient in some way if I ask for help. While it's important for my village to feel appreciated, it's of equal importance that those around me know it as well.

When you seek support, it is not because you are failing. When you add to your village, it is not because you are incapable or are lacking in skill to do it yourself. When you seek help and welcome such support into your life, you are acknowledging your potential and putting the team in place so you can realize it to its fullest measure. You are empowering yourself to achieve the next lofty goal ahead. You are ensuring your children are supported in meeting their potential. You are building a village which not only makes the impossible, possible, but will offer a level of love and care as a collective. Much like the expression, *"Two heads are better than one,"* it's reasonable to think more loving hearts around our children would also be of value and benefit. If a house is made a home by the love that fills it, then guilt has no place as we invite more love into it.

Alongside our daily thoughts, we must also accept none of us have all the answers. There will be days we have some answers, and we will have many moments where our experiences will support us in knowing what to do. Outside of that, we are all doing the best we can and hopefully being a friend to others in helping them do the same. When receiving a compliment related to parenting, my standard (and truthful) response is that I'll only know decades from now, when my children are older, if I was on the right course. If anyone pretends to know otherwise, run for the hills. What I do know with absolute certainty, however, is that the things you love most in the various facets of your life should never be lined with guilt. Whether you love starting your day with a morning run, enjoy meeting a friend for lunch, or attending an evening course, don't assess what a mile, maintaining a friendship, or advancing your education is worth compared to time with your children. When they see you loving something for yourself, they will be inspired to develop such an interest or seek out their own passions.

My four-year-old, Claire, often asks for her blazer, puts miscellaneous business cards in her cubby at pre-school and holds "meetings" with her stuffed toys. As I cook dinner, my five-year-old, Leah, will line up chairs, seat her dolls, and tell a story of where they are all flying to on this evening's business trip. They also love dancing and singing (both of which I have no talent or hope for improvement), skiing and horses (two things I'll love for all of my life), and next year will bring more interests; some related to me and others that will not be. By showing immense dedication and love for a part of your life that belongs only to you, you are exemplifying to those around you that you deserve to have such things in your life and will inspire them to search out the same for themselves. In my experience, my children, by extension, love pieces of my life that I love so much, regardless of whether those pieces are ones we can share together or if they take us apart from one another. They are not resentful or jealous. They are curious and excited to learn more about the interests, loves, and passions of those around them.

There is so much in life worthy of celebration; take the time to revel in all that you are doing in yours. Rather than unrealistically striving for perfect and permanent balance, accept that you can become comfortable with the reality of conflict. Admit to yourself and others that you may not always be there to capture every moment, but be grateful you have your village to celebrate them in your absence. Trade in guilt for acceptance; the sacrifices you make are what allow for the possibilities in your life. You deserve to love a piece of your life that's only for you, and in doing so, you teach your children that they deserve the same.

So to all of you superstar moms, stop striving for the impossible and be proud of yourself for the same reasons your children will be so very proud of you.

~ To my parents with love: Thank you for surrounding me with an incredible community throughout my childhood - it is what has inspired me to create the same for my own children.

13

EMPOWERING YOUR PREGNANCY

by Caitlyn Laird

"You are never a lost cause, but a seedling preparing to bloom."

Caitlyn Laird

Caitlyn Laird is a first time mom to Isla (born June 2017), fur-parent to their dog, Kacy, and wife to Alex. Originally from a small town in Ontario, now living in Halifax, Nova Scotia, she works in dentistry and network marketing. Her love for people has been the motivation behind her success in customer service. Caitlyn loves nothing more than to laugh, so naturally, she is drawn to those with a colourful and sarcastic sense of humour.

As an optimist, she always looks for the positive side of things when faced with trials. She is all about making bold choices and standing out from the crowd. As a very passionate person, Caitlyn strives to help others in anyway she can, and volunteers in her community most weekends. She also uses her spare time to get crafty, adventure outdoors, and spend time with her loved ones. Living a healthy lifestyle is a priority in her life, and she endeavors to help others feel and look their best. She may be a dreamer, but is determined to make her dreams a reality.

Motherhood is still a new chapter in her life, but she is fully embracing it and views every day as a gift.

ig: @imstillnotlyon | t: @CaitlynLaird

"A woman experiencing an unplanned pregnancy
also deserves to experience unplanned joy."
~ Patricia Heaton

I N 2011, FORTY-FIVE PERCENT of all pregnancies in the United States were unintended. By age forty-five, more than half of all US women will have had an unintended pregnancy.[5] When you think about it, those numbers are pretty mind-blowing. So chances are, either you or someone you know has had a "surprise" baby. When you think of a surprise, you normally think of a surprise party or finding a $10 bill at the bottom of your purse. Two very positive things. But a surprise pregnancy can be a completely different story. Most people will say that they were terrified or in shock when they found out that their bodies were growing a little-uninvited human. That's exactly where I was in October 2016. It was a Monday morning, and I was a week late. *I'll just take a pregnancy test, just in case. But I'm sure I'm not pregnant,* I said to myself. Even though there was a fifty percent chance that the stick was going to be positive, I was mentally not prepared for that answer. *Nope, no way.* Guess what, it was. I was in major denial, so I went and bought a pack of two pregnancy tests. Guess what, BOTH POSITIVE.

That's the moment where I lost it. Shaking, with tears pouring down my cheeks, I went back to my desk with a pale face. I couldn't

5 Finer LB and Zolna MR. (n.d). *Declines in Unintended pregnancy in the United States, 2008-2011*, New England Journal of Medicine, 2016, 374(9) : 843-852, Retrieved from: http://www.nejm.org/doi/full/10.1056/NEJMsa1506575

even speak the words to my husband. So I texted him a picture of the test, which is something I really regret, but the moment when I saw those two lines, the panic set in and it felt like my heart stopped. I didn't feel ready - the thought of labor terrified me and I didn't know how to take care of a baby. I was scared of the changes this pregnancy would bring about; I didn't think we could take on the financial burden, and I love my sleep. There were so many "what if's" racing through my mind, and I became my own worst enemy. To make things worse, I felt guilty for not being excited about this child. It took me a solid two weeks to smile again because I was drowning myself in doubt and worry. I can honestly say I was devastated. Up until that moment, I never envisioned myself as a mother. I came from a small immediate family with only one brother who was almost three years younger than me, and most of my cousins were older than me, so my experience with children primarily came from working as a receptionist at a dental office. Every day, I saw kids who were throwing tantrums, screaming, biting, and puking, although to be fair, they were at the dentist, so you can't blame them for not being happy about it. My patience had run dry, and I was so happy to go home to my quiet life. Even when I was a kid, I didn't take much interest in babies; I was more interested in animals (crazy dog lady in the making). I never did catch baby fever, my ambitions and dreams of traveling were the Tylenol to that fever.

My husband, Alex, on the other hand, is the definition of a "kid person." He knows exactly how to communicate, play, handle kids, and actually enjoy it. Despite this, he wasn't exactly thrilled with the timing of this pregnancy, but he dealt with the news way better than I did, that's for sure. It was funny because, for the longest time, Alex thought I was playing a cruel joke on him (seriously, I had to pee on a pregnancy test in front of him before he believed me). He still managed to bring me back down to earth, and he helped me to see that this wasn't the end of the world. Instead, it was a positive step forward in our marriage. Just because this pregnancy was not planned, does not mean that this child would be unwanted. Of course, it could have taken place at a more convenient time for us, but our circumstances could have been so much worse. It is easy to feel sorry for yourself and sit on the couch feeling hopeless. But what kind of life is that? Where is that going to get you? It may not feel like it at the time, but you can take control of your life.

In my experience, it may take you some time to wrap your head around your life switching gears so drastically, but there are some things you can do to rise above the smoke even without the support of a spouse.

Get educated. If this is your first pregnancy, you might lack confidence in your childbearing / parenting abilities like I did. We are so lucky to live in a time with so many freaking resources for information available to us at the tips of our fingers. The more knowledge you gain, the more confidence you will have, and the happier you'll likely be. Be prepared for the unsolicited advice people will throw at you because it's coming for you like mosquitoes swarming you at your weekend barbeque. I was polite - I listened, nodded, and faked a smile, but at the end of the day, I was doing my research and making my own decisions. You don't have to make decisions based solely on other moms' personal experiences. What works for one parent / child may not work for the rest. Not to mention, recommendations from the American Academy of Pediatrics (AAP) change quite often. Personally, I prefer to follow current and updated information, but to each their own. Do you! There are some great apps that you can download onto your mobile device that track your pregnancy each week, tell you what symptoms to expect, update you with the development progress of your baby, and connect you to other mommies. My favorite app that I used during my pregnancy was Glow Nurture because it had so much valuable information, and it was straightforward to use. The more I learned about what my body was doing to create this little human, the more fascinating and exciting my experience became. It is indeed amazing what our bodies are capable of, and it is so much fun to learn about it.

Take it one day at a time. Your life has suddenly changed forever. You are allowed to feel overwhelmed; I'd be concerned if you didn't. You are going to have to make a lot of important and challenging decisions. But just like a thousand piece puzzle, it's going to take some time to put the pieces of your life back together. I had a tough time with this one because I tend to overthink pretty much everything and this, in turn, prevented me from enjoying some of my pregnancy. Once I was able to accept that I wasn't going to have all the answers right away, I was finally able to go about my days without the burning feeling of anxiety in my chest when I thought about my future. I knew everything would fall into place eventually; so by focusing on present issues, I was slowly placing those puzzle pieces in a peaceful frame of mind. Think about what you have to do today, not tomorrow or next week, but today. If you are finding that you're plagued with anxiety over not being ready for your baby's arrival, do something small every day to get prepared. Those small accomplishments satisfied me enough that when I put my head down at night, I had something to be proud of. Making this a routine helped me to extinguish that wildfire of anxiety. Of course, if your anxiety is preventing you from being able to accomplish daily tasks, it's time to get your butt to your doctor.

Start a project. I cannot emphasize enough how helpful distraction was for me. Call me Granny, but one I found to be very therapeutic was knitting. According to HealthFitnessRevolution.org knitting can, "effectively relieve stress because it allows you to focus on the task in front of you rather than dwelling in a perpetual cycle of stress." Knitting may not be your thing, but that's okay because there are an endless amount of possibilities to suit you. One activity which is both fun and productive is to work on the nursery. Pinterest will be your best friend. There are so many cost effective do it yourself (DIY) projects on there which will help you get your nursery organized, personalized, and functional. I found that during my pregnancy, all I ever talked about was my pregnancy. Not because I really wanted to, but rather, that was just the conversation other people would bring up. I couldn't blame them because people are typically excited to talk about their pregnancy, but I was just sick of talking about it! Sometimes, I felt that I needed to get my mind off it because it was consuming my life. I couldn't exactly go out and have a couple of drinks to relax and forget about my worries temporarily, so having a project to work on really got me through those days where I just wanted to escape. There's a certain level of satisfaction which goes hand in hand with a completed project. When you can say, "I painted this room," or "I knitted that baby hat," it can be a serious confidence booster.

Take care of yourself. You've probably heard this before - eat healthy, get some exercise, get enough sleep. Those things are all essential for the physical health of you and of your little peanut because your body is busy creating a person, but it's not enough. According to the Mayo Clinic, using relaxation techniques can have many positive health benefits such as reducing the activity of stress hormones, lowering blood pressure, improving digestion and reducing muscle tension and chronic pain.[6] What helps you relax? I live in Halifax, Canada, which is a beautiful, waterfront city. Something that helped me zone out was going for a walk by the ocean. There's something about breathing in that salty air, feeling the cool breeze on my face which helped bring serenity to my anxious, sleep-deprived mind. No ocean? No problem. Put some coconut oil in your hair, a DIY mask on your face, and drink that mocktail your friend told you about. That's right, pamper yourself ladies, it's important for your sanity. Trust me, take advantage of your freedom while you can because once you have a newborn, you'll consider yourselves lucky to get a shower. I was having a really hard time falling asleep at night, most nights, I'd be up until 2am with my brain doing laps. So I took my issue to a Facebook pregnancy support group, and someone had suggested trying yoga exercises. Amy Lynch at mindbodygreen.com states, "Studies have suggested that practicing yoga while pregnant can also improve sleep, reduce stress and anxiety, increase the strength, flexibility, and endurance of muscles needed for childbirth." It really did help me to sleep better and trust me, you're going to want to have those muscles ready for labor. Do all the Kegels! Pushing a baby out is no joke. If I could do anything differently, I would have set a reminder on my phone to tell me to do Kegels. Your life revolves around that baby growing inside of you, but take care of you, for you. Give in to those weird pregnancy cravings once in a while! Take a day off from work and do whatever it is you want to do. You're not just a baby factory. You matter as a person. Please don't forget that.

Ask for help. At some point in our lives in general, we all need help. When you find yourself to be unexpectedly pregnant and you're already struggling to get your own crap together, you WILL need help. When I called my mom to tell her that I was with child, it's an understatement to say I was emotionally unstable. Hearing her voice assure me that everything was going to be okay was exactly what I needed to calm down. I was fortunate enough to have a fantastic support team, and they were vital in keeping my sanity in check. If you have a support system in place to support you, take advantage of it. They are there

....

6   The Mayo Clinic. (2017, April 19). *Relaxation Techniques, Try These Steps to Reduce Stress.* Retrieved from: https://www.mayoclinic.org/healthy-lifestyle/stress-management/in-depth/relaxation-technique/art-20045368?pg=1

because they love you, and because they want to be there to help you. If you don't have anyone who you can dump your crap on, make an effort to create contacts because we all need emotional support as our hormones are wreaking havoc inside our bodies. We live on a planet with seven billion other people, and you only really need a couple of those to link arms with. There are lots of other mamas out there looking to connect, so you are never, ever alone.

Whatever your current situation may be, you've got this! The beauty of life is that change can happen within a blink of an eye - it's always interesting and keeps us on our toes. But for a moment in time, my pregnancy did not seem to be like a good kind of change. Why? Because I was only focusing on the challenges ahead and letting the negativity brew and fester. Self-doubt consumed me that first trimester because I just did not feel worthy or capable of having this child. The truth is, at that time, I really had no way of knowing what challenges I would actually face. As Karen Salmansohn said, *"If you ever find your-self doubting you can make it through a challenge, simply think back to everything you've overcome in the past."* I wish I had read this quote on that Monday morning.

Seriously, take a minute to reflect on hardships that you've faced, and how you lived to tell the tale. You are stronger and more capable than you think you are, I promise you that. Life has a way of sorting itself out even when you can't see how it will happen. I wish that there was a way to get a small glimpse of the future because I would have seen a woman that has experienced such happiness and love. I would have seen a happy, healthy, beautiful baby girl who owns the hearts of every-one she meets. I would have learned that I had nothing to be afraid of, because every single challenge that came my way, I would do it willingly over and over again to have the life that I have now. I was afraid that my life would be over because of the limitations that we now had, but in reality, this child has opened up a whole new world of experiences and joy. No, my life is not perfect. But it's still mine.

~ I dedicate this chapter to my loving husband, Alex, and my beautiful daughter, Isla, for teaching me what the true meaning of love really is.

14

THE SLEEPING TREE

by Janice Meredith

"The worst thing ever happened. I came out a stronger woman and mother".

Janice Meredith

Having flourished in the pages of women's fashion, Janice loves to assess the best designer runway trends for women and men and demonstrate how to bring them to life in the real world. On top of possessing a natural talent for shopping and a passion for fashion, Janice is also blessed with a keen eye for finding that "just right" item.

Janice's positioning on fashion is all about crafting personal confidence through individual style. Her segments on Cityline not only educate viewers on how to unearth style that highlights the most fashionable and confident side of each of us, but she also expertly coaches around pairing items to create a well-rounded but minimal wardrobe.

In addition to covering multiple aspects of fashion and personal style, Janice has also written extensively about beauty, décor, travel and all things fabulous prior to her move to television. Currently, Janice is an on-air fashion and lifestyle expert for Cityline, as well as being a go-to expert for various news outlets.

Her obsession with style is exceeded only by her passion for her four busy children, from whom she gathers daily inspiration - fashion-wise and otherwise.

www.Janicemeredith.com
ig: @Janicemeredithstyle
fb: janice.meredith.style
t: @Janicemw

"I am not what happened to me. I am what I choose to become."
~ Carl Jung

I STEP OUTSIDE MY HOUSE ON A SUNNY SPRING DAY, lock the door behind me, and wait. Soon my smiling husband comes striding up to the front door. But I don't allow him to advance. Instead, I hand him his car key and cellphone, declaring that he is no longer welcome in our house. My house now.

In a time that is supposed to be quiet and child-free, I have planned on resting while my husband takes our two kids to the park. Being five months pregnant with twins tires me out by mid-afternoon, but today, I'm restless, so I putter around our home. That's when I move his blackberry to tidy up and discover it's unlocked which is not allowed by his employer. I'll admit it's been an unusual month since we found out we were pregnant with twins, but I chalked it up to overwhelming shock and stress. Discovering emails detailing a whole life with another woman is like a massive wall of pain hitting my entire body.

The fight or flight mode has kicked in, and I decided to fight instead. He chose to end this marriage when he went outside our relationship, so I'm doing what he was too weak to do. And that brings me to our porch where I meet him, my husband of twelve years at our door. I turn him away and lock myself inside where I fall to the ground. Finally allowing myself to succumb to the realization of his betrayal.

Spanning the twenty minutes from finding the disgusting emails to locking him out of my house, I hastily send SOS emails. One friend met my two children as they returned from the park and led them off to a playdate, away from the wreckage. Other friends responded and arrived quickly assembling into the role of my village. They help me off the floor where they found me gasping for air, arms wrapped around my belly.

Moving forward into action, they begin packing his things up. I gather my strength to get up and walk around my house. It's silent except for the soft crinkle of the plastic bags being filled. No one talks to me, but they do look at me. Watching me. I can feel their eyes, but I'm afraid to confront their looks. I don't want to answer their questions. I'm overwhelmed by my own.

Eventually, my kids return from their play date, and somehow I tuck them into bed without them having any knowledge of the day's tragedies. In the morning, we join friends for brunch. The kids playing is a welcomed distraction. My friends have conversed through the night and morning, so my assembled village is up to date and now in motion. Plans have been made, shifts allocated, and appointments booked. I feel overwhelmed by all the attention and then I realize, it's Mother's Day.

Even being surrounded by a loving family and a supportive village, the void remains vast. It's a gaping hole which needs to be mended before my twins are born. Pain that needs to be managed so I can love my kids who deserve so much more than what has been thrown at them. I feel logical steps will keep me moving forward to becoming Janice again. I don't know what my future holds, and the uncertainty is frightening, so I grasp at what gives me even the smallest sense of control.

My birth plan had been to cab it to the hospital. Stealth like, in the middle of the night, with no one to fuss over me. Just arrive at the hospital, push out a couple of babies with the help of some matter of fact nursing staff, and then go home. I wanted to shed that image I felt everyone had of me that I was that woman whose husband cheated on her while she was pregnant with twins. Everyone in my neighborhood knew this story. I was done with being an urban myth, and hoped having the babies under the radar would keep any attention off my situation, and even more so, my shame.

My sister would never forgive me if she wasn't there for the delivery. She had been such a remarkable pillar of strength and wisdom. Present without judgment and overflowing with such enthusiasm over these two innocent babies. Determined to welcome these boys into a world where we could change previously accepted behavior, my sister reassured me of my own strength and power, as a woman, and mainly as a mother; that I was more than capable of raising my children and they would learn to respect and appreciate females. She was the first one to give me a glimpse of my future.

My village was so excited about the world having two more boys and didn't see any shame in my tragedy. The real problem, in their eyes, was my husband's behavior and treatment of the situation, which was in no way reflective of me. Ever so slowly, I began to understand this.

One Sunday afternoon, at the end of August, my twin boys finally arrived, and I officially became a single mother of four young children. In my worldview, that's not how families were supposed to be. I had been married, lived in a lovely house on a pretty street with the goal of creating a big, beautiful family. Babies are such amazing beings who should be surrounded by intense love and care. I found myself in the hospital surrounded by loving new dads gushing over their babies which worsened my feelings of loneliness. Here, I feared I couldn't do this alone. *Four children outnumbered two parents, so how would I manage this?* Somehow, I was quickly surrounded by friends and family. They took turns bringing me food to eat and food for my soul. My village ooh-ing and aah-ing over my babies was something I felt they deserved. Seeing all this love was what I needed. It didn't matter where it came from - love is love, and my friends showered us with it. I wasn't ever alone as my sister stayed with me during the nights, and friends streamed through during the days. I made it through my hospital stay rewriting my definition of what my family was now resembling and began to bridge the gaping hole where my partner should have been, but was no longer.

I began to feel it would work. These moments slowly brought me joy, which meant I was healing and able to feel once again. I had asked for help and in return, received a world of love and support.

Growing up in a childhood playing the role of caretaker to my parents, before moving into marriage and taking care of my husband, I was quite adept at being the caregiver. When the divorce and pain were too hard to process, I reverted to simply taking care of others, in this case, my children, my friends, and my clients. It pushed me through each day until I was exhausted for sleep. And sleep I would. My daily goal was to get so tired that I wouldn't wake up in the middle of the night for it was in those moments where I honestly felt alone, small, and unprepared.

Every few nights, I would lay in bed so exhausted, but unable to sleep, and that's when my mind would run wild. I would recall the good memories and dwell on what exactly happened to get me there. My mind would spin wild with questions; questions which I would never know the answers to. I didn't need to go down that rabbit hole. I had to consciously remind myself that none of this was my doing. It was his. I couldn't own his actions or mistakes, nor could I question what I believed was the life I was living. Rewriting the past wasn't the answer. I had to trust I had lived the life I had been presented with. And now, it was new and just different. The sooner I accepted this, the quicker my mental anguish would diminish.

By morning, I would wake up and start my day again. I stopped planning ahead excessively. My situation changed daily. What I could or couldn't handle was based on how many components were affecting me on any given day. What nearly crushed me one day, didn't break me on another day. Some days, I was moved to tears, while I had other days where I could smile through whatever came my way. Planning a future had set expectations that led to my devastation. From now on, approaching each day on a "one day at a time" basis would allow me to stay present, instead of obsessively focusing on a future that was beyond my control, and give me the freedom to adapt as things changed.

Christmas came, and I went all out with a full, grand tree. One that I would set up in the family room where we could enjoy it. Not a small proper tree placed prominently in the front window for all the neighbors to see. I picked out the new tree, carried it into the house, and got it upright in the stand. So magnificent that it scratched the crisp white ceiling and snaked its way for a few inches. I strung lights and adorned it with boxes of new decorations. As I sat with the kids, enjoying the lights, my beautiful tree fell over shattering decorations and spilling water everywhere. "Not a problem," I said to the kids. We carried on with our evening, and once they were in bed, I tackled righting our tree. But I couldn't get it back up. It was too big for my stand.

Days went by, and I simply did not look at the tree. I didn't have the strength or energy to fix it. I understood the problem, but couldn't do anything about it. I was so upset; I couldn't even think of a solution. One of my kids shared with a neighbor that our tree was sleeping which was the exact word I was using! Later that night, her husband showed up to help. One quick look at the situation and he left to buy a new, bigger tree stand. Something so simple evaded me in my shame of not being able to fix my problem or ask for help.

I learned if I looked at each day as one day at a time, it wasn't so scary. One day at a time, I could handle. There was a schedule with kids, and I could follow that for the majority of my day and intersperse it with small "Janice" things. Eventually, those mere moments grew to chunks of time where I came out a bit more put together. I took every opportunity that came to me to be busy which granted me trying new things. Initially, I took these on as a distraction, but it soon became a way to start building my new future, my new self.

Those mid sleep wake-ups had me fearful of having no control. And in my mind, I equated control with success. I could control very little, so whatever I could control, I did it well. My house was my domain now. I took every opportunity to make it mine. It didn't matter if it was a thrift store find or a discount retailer purchase, it quickly came together as a very strong reflection of who I was becoming. I sold my lovely matching bedroom furniture and threw my new mattress on the floor, and instead, I used an old change table as my dresser and put mismatched baskets it in. There was nothing pretty or perfect about it, but I loved it. This new freedom from the constraints of who I once thought I was, and who I was supposed to be, fell away. And I flourished.

That first Christmas however, challenged my growth. The twins would spend the night with their dad for the very first time since our separation. As all four kids left with their father, I was barely able to contain my sobs. My beaming, encouraging smile quickly melted into a quivering mess. I had a whole afternoon and night to myself, and it was Christmas. Previously, this was a time where I happily hosted family and friends at our house. And now, I was utterly alone in this big house with no one to mother. And over at my ex-husband's home, *she* would be staying over to "help" with the kids. I started to wonder how they would explain this to the older two. This was my first attempt at trying not to parent the other household which included not asking questions or wondering what happens during their day. I couldn't. It was just too hard.

Unable to know how I would feel or what to expect, I couldn't sort out how I wanted to spend this holiday. My village made plans that they felt might work if they were in my situation. In an effort not to be alone, I followed along with their plans but my first dinner was still two hours from now. But my first dinner was still two hours before I was to arrive. Someone else's holiday chaos might be the perfect distraction to my child-free arms. Waiting, I wandered through my house, lost in the silence. I couldn't look around as everywhere I turned, I saw my babies. I needed to clean our Christmas morning mess. Very pointedly, I stacked their presents and picked up the torn wrapping paper and debris like I was a racehorse with blinders. The logic proved to be very helpful. Soon, the gifts were piled up and recycling bags filled.

Now what? I asked myself. I drew a blank on things I could do, and soon the inevitable sadness rose up in me again. I didn't want to be this weak, weepy thing. I worked so hard to be strong, but right now, I felt deflated and sad.

Tightening my imaginary blinders, I walked upstairs right past the kids' rooms and into mine. I needed to have a shower. I have learned that these provide many benefits: a place to do the ugly cry, a warm haven to wrap myself up in, the very obvious clean factor, and a chance to exit with a fresh perspective.

Needless to say, I shower a lot. Sometimes more than once a day. I am completely okay with this unique form of self-therapy.

For those first three years, I focused mostly on my kids where I felt comfortable and needed. I had a skilled therapist who helped with addressing the betrayal and guiding my healing process to ensure I can trust and love again. She also helped with the parenting struggles I encountered while learning how to co-parent with a strong-willed ex-husband. I listened to my lawyer who guided me through the divorce process as she had no emotional baggage, but simply the goal of getting a fair and reasonable divorce. I listened to my friends - their opinions and personalities were spread across the spectrum from those who vehemently touted I was better off without him, to those who were there to listen and empathize. Then there were others - the ones I called to reminisce and dissect my past or to distract myself and carry on like this wasn't my current life situation. All the above aspects were a crucial part of my healing and growth.

I learned that I mattered; I had a voice and a place. While others were helping me, I cultivated new components for my redefined self. I discovered that I was needed, and had many great things of value to offer.

I have never looked back with regret at locking that door. My confidence in trusting my instinct propels me to build my family in the new way I have envisioned for us. And for me, my fears are minimal, as the worst thing I could have ever imagined, happened. Not only did I survive it, but I came out a much stronger, deeper, and more aware woman, and mother. In the end, he is just one man. I will not allow one man to destroy me or rule me. Life is to be a journey made up of chapters - each one bringing with it lessons and growth of its own. I constantly work hard towards closing this chapter, excited for every new page.

~ My heart and soul are constantly fed by my children: Keeley, Ronan, Lachlan, and Conall. They supply constant joy and love, providing each day with a fresh viewpoint. I thank my sister who has unequivocally supported me with sheer love as her guide. My village has been there from the moment we met in passing to talk blazers, shoes, handbags, or carrots. Each one is unique in their character and therefore our relationships are truly individual. Yet as a whole, we are unwavering in our mutual respect and support for each other. We bring love, laughter, and wine without question or judgement. As a posse, we raise each other to a higher degree of our best selves with compassion and best wishes.

15

WHERE IS
MY VILLAGE?

by Neli Tavares Hession

"If you ever feel
alone and excluded,
remember your
village is out there."

Neli Tavares Hession

Neli Tavares Hession is a mind, body, and spirit wellness coach and founder of MamaZen Coaching. She is a board certified holistic wellness practitioner with a concentration in holistic nutrition from Southwest Institute of Healing Arts as well as a holistic life coach from the University of Wellness. She is a reiki level I practitioner and Barbell Project ambassador through *Gorgo Magazine*.

Neli is married and lives on Rhode Island with her four children. She enjoys meditation, fitness, nature, and new experiences. When she isn't busy being a mom and running girls empowerment workshops, she can be found working for her clients at Nelihession.com, as well as Facebook and Instagram.

www.nelihession.com
ig: @neli_hession
fb: neli.hession

"Moms are one of two things — supported or exhausted.
The supported ones have grandmas and grandpas showing up
and cooking or giving them date nights or appointment time or a
full night's sleep. They have aunts and uncles, best friends with kids,
neighbors with kids and yards, playgroups, babysitter connections.
The exhausted ones… they look more like me…"
~ Liane Cole

WE ARE A FAMILY OF SIX. My husband and I live in a crazy, chaotic, and LOUD household with four wildly active children. We have the smorgasbord of milestones all happening under one roof with a teenager, a pre-teen, a five-year-old, and a tornado of a three-year-old. Oh, and a six-year-old dog that still thinks she is a puppy. Trust me when I say, this house is *never* quiet or still for too long.

So why did I feel so **alone**?

I didn't always feel this isolated and alone. And the ironic thing is, the isolation didn't creep in at baby #1 or even baby #2. Oddly enough, the dark, echo of the lonely tunnel hit me shortly after I had my third child.

Up until that point in my journey of motherhood, I had all the fanfare that comes to you seemingly naturally when you have your first baby. People nearly broke down my door to see a glimpse of that precious little one, and they would bring food for the tired mom and dad, and gifts of diapers and cute outfits for the every ridiculously growing infant. There were constant streams of offers of babysitting so mommy and daddy could have a night out to feel like adults again, or sleep in and catch up on that much-needed rest. It seemed that those around me always knew what I needed and were more than happy and willing to jump through hoops to help.

At that time, I didn't fully appreciate what I had. Partly because I didn't think there was a darker alternative - I really did think that everyone got this sort of red carpet treatment when they had a child. After all, it is what you see on tv and read on Facebook all the time. And also, because I'm very much an introvert and crave space, when all this attention was pouring in, I naturally retreated and recoiled a bit. You know that saying, *"You don't know what you got 'til it's gone."* Yeah, well that hit me like a ton of bricks when I had my third child.

When my son, Brady, came onto the scene, the fanfare seemed to come to a screeching halt. No fault of my amazing little dude in the least! It was just the timing of things. Baby #1, it's all well and good when you have the quintessential "normal" white picket fence type of household with the 1.5 kids and a dog. But when you get into the three, four, or more kid scenario, people sort of treat you like a circus freak. At least, that was my perception of it. And, naturally, it is hard for others, who may already have their hands full with their own lives, to now try and juggle your soccer team of a household in an attempt to babysit your children. And people naturally assume you are really busy (which you are), so I think the tendency is to leave you alone and "not get in your way" so you can tend to your motherly duties as best you can. Most folks don't realize that just about everyone you know is doing that, thus leaving you alone, where you start hearing your voice echo "Hello?" down that dark, lonely tunnel of motherhood.

After baby #3, family dynamics changed with our extended family, leaving everyone less than enthused with even seeing one another for a while, let alone wanting to extend that olive branch to help in any way.

I had also lost my job shortly after giving birth to my son; a place, which I didn't realize at the time, served as an outlet to express myself, still feel connected to other humans, and to share motherhood stories with other fellow moms. All these things, I didn't realize it then, were a factor in keeping me afloat. I felt important and **included** while at work - with colleagues sitting with you during your lunch break, the constant buzz of a busy office, and the phone calls with other humans to chat with. When all of that came to an end, I had no idea how lonely and isolated I would really feel.

I dreamed of the days when my friends would come over and visit, bring casseroles, and share some cool stories. When I initially got the crushing news of losing my job, I quickly looked on the bright side and envisioned going to the baby yoga drop-in classes and meeting other moms; finding instant bonds and going for walks around the neighborhood with our babies happily napping in their strollers. I was certain that in a few months' time, I would have shoulders to cry on, hands to hold, and a house full of laughter.

But as the months wore on, the stress of losing my job caused stress in my marriage. Motherhood has a way of making you feel like you lost a sense of yourself in a way, and now, without that "fancy title" of the business world, I was really lost. At that same time, my husband got a promotion and was really living his dream. Oddly enough, I started to resent him for it. I felt like everything got taken away from me, and he didn't get it. *How could he?!* He still got to be HIM through all of this. And he was even able to become a "better" version of himself on top of everything with his new fancy job. That feeling of resentment and jealousy toward him certainly caught me by surprise. In all honesty, his job promotion was a blessing during a time where we would have had to struggle with our surprise situation of having three children and being reliant on one income. I was supposed to feel proud of him, especially since I knew how hard he had worked to get to that point in his career. But instead, I loathed him. He didn't have to stay home all day wiping butts, cleaning boogers, and dealing with the never-ending crying and carpooling of older siblings to various places. I wanted to have a successful career too. I wanted to feel like "somebody," but instead, I felt like a nobody.

Don't get me wrong, motherhood is more than a full-time job and can be (and is), really rewarding in its own magical way. Throughout the years, I had been a stay at home mom for a few years, I worked full-time day jobs while my children went to daycare for a few years, and even juggled second and third shift jobs so I could be at home - stay at home mommy by day and working mommy by night. I believe I have honestly, and FULLY experienced every aspect of juggling motherhood, life, and work, and can see how each one has its challenges as well as its own hidden beauty.

But something about this journey this time around was so different.

In the past, I still had family and friends around me. I had people willing to help me juggle it all if I couldn't leave work to pick up a sick child from daycare, or if I needed to run some errands and my schedule with work and kids' activities were jam-packed.

If I was home with the kids, the doorbell wouldn't stop ringing, the phone was constantly buzzing with texts and messages from friends and family.

This time around, when I asked for help, naturally everyone was busy. And those who were left, who could and wanted to help - I felt bad for leaning on them too much, so I stopped asking. I stopped reaching out; I stopped everything and withdrew deeper into a dark hole.

Anytime I briefly ran into someone at the market or out while running errands, I dodged them. Again, partly because I'm naturally introverted, but now more so, because I felt ashamed. I was stuck in a house all day and not doing much of anything as far as personal growth, so I had nothing to talk about with people.

Cue in, more avoidance of friends and family, and unresolved postpartum depression.

I was a big ball of resentment and anger by day... and sneaky bouts of crying myself to sleep at night. The deeper I sank into this dark hole, the more I avoided people, and the more I truly believed they were avoiding me. Depression has a sneaky way of changing our perception of things quite dramatically sometimes.

Four years passed, and then I had my fourth child, Owen. I had a better grip on my depression thanks to my meditation practices and nutrition overhaul. However, I was slightly sideswiped by my new son's speech delay. I needed to attend appointments with specialists and doctors and keep visitations with Child Outreach coordinators organized. I needed sleep. I needed a shower. I needed a hug. I needed to breathe. I needed someone to lean on and tell me things were going to be okay with my son. I needed to hear stories from other women close to me that they were perhaps experiencing the same things and how all was well - I needed a village badly. Someone besides my husband, because one man cannot carry the weight of a whole village.

With this new bump in the road, I quickly realized how much I needed to stretch beyond my comfort zone and reach out to as many moms, and mom groups as I could. The anxiety and worry about my son's social and emotional well-being was too much of a weight to take on alone. I attended as many mom-and-kid programs my city had to offer. I spent as many hours at playgrounds, play gyms, and community centers as this introverted mom could bear. I talked to every mom I could muster up a conversation with at the school pick up line. Each time, I would put on a brave face and try to connect, but came away empty-handed. It reminded me of those high school days of trying to find a seat in the cafeteria and never quite fitting in. Everywhere I turned, seemingly, no one had any room for new village members.

It wasn't until Brady started preschool that I found my village. And by that point, I had stopped trying. Preschool drop-offs and pickups were just like my other two children before. Most of the time, I was either rushing or running late. Most of the time, I either needed a shower, or I looked disheveled. Sometimes I had forgotten to pack homework, a class project, or a lunch. I was, what I dubbed as a "hot mess mom." Over the years, I blamed my "hot mess-ness" for possibly not being accepted into other mom villages. I was also sarcastic, and my sense of humor could be perceived as "off color." Other moms appeared to be well put together, prim and proper. No wonder I was "rejected." I was an outcast. But I wasn't changing for anyone. I continued to be myself and those who couldn't accept that, were just no longer a part of my life, I guess.

Cue in the "Bad News Bears." This was a group of preschool moms that hung around after class let out and allowed their children to play together outside. Rain, snow, cold, or sunshine - it didn't matter; they were there watching the kids run around and get dirty without a care in the world.

One day, as I was walking past them (technically RUSHING past them so I could hurry and get Brady in the car and avoid social interaction), one of the moms yelled out to me, "Hey, aren't you going to let Brady play today?" My mind quickly rushed to everything I had to tend to back home. In my mind, I had thousands of things to accomplish before my husband came home from work to prove I was a productive housewife. Hanging around after school was not on my to-do list. Brady was so excited to play with his friends that I caved and let him play along with his little brother, Owen.

I was worried at first about allowing Owen into the mix. These were well-behaved kids, and Owen was my "loose cannon." Along with his speech delay, he had aggression that came out of nowhere. I nicknamed him "Hulk" because he truly was like the Hulk. Fine one minute, but the littlest thing could set him off at any moment, and watch out if you were on the receiving end of that anger.

I was worried Owen would lash out at one of the other kids and that would be the end of everyone's playdate. And possibly be the end of me being included in a group, finally.

As the moms stood and kept a loose eye on the kids playing, they openly chatted about life. Motherhood. And how it wasn't all roses and sunshine. Their off-color jokes about motherhood were eerily reminiscent of mine. Their sarcasm was a breath of fresh air!

As the school months wore on, these after-school playdates were a natural given. We all looked forward to it, not just the kids, but as moms, we NEEDED this time to release our burdens, stressors, and worries. And it helped to have others commiserate or offer a similar story to let the each other know we aren't alone in this. We quickly found out our children had similar personalities, social and emotional issues, or speech delays. The more these playdates happened, the more I realized these moms were going through exactly what I had been going through with Owen. And Owen learned how to play well with other kids. He needed this group just as much as I did.

This group of moms dubbed themselves "The Bad News Bears," after we all openly chatted about how all of us felt excluded from other mom cliques. We found out how all of us felt rejected or excluded, and perhaps it may have been our "hot mess-ness" or sarcasm that others just didn't get. Or maybe it was because our children weren't "perfect." But our kids were perfect to us, and we were great moms in our own right. We all bonded over our imperfections. It felt like a huge weight lifted off our shoulders knowing that we didn't have to pretend to have our shit together to fit in. We didn't have to put ourselves out there and get rejected any longer by other mom cliques. We were a band of misfits who loved and appreciated one another.

In those months of being a part of the "Bad News Bears," I thrived so much more, both as a person and a mother. I learned so much more about Owen and the services available to help him and us for his speech. I also learned although Owen may be fine and he may outgrow his speech issues, if at all I was worried or had a concern creep up, I had a band of misfits to lean on and make me feel okay with the world again.

It may have taken me ten plus years to find my village, but I found them, and they were everything I needed and more! Exactly as I needed them - sarcasm, messiness, and all. If you ever feel alone and excluded, just remember your village is out there. It may take a while to bump into them, but they are out there. Trust that you will find yours.

Until you find them, hang in there, Mama, you've got this!

> ~ To my self-created tiny village, Adriana, Maggie, Brady, and Owen: Four of the most magical beings I know. Thank you for always being mommy's cheerleaders. You make me brave enough to always do big things. Thank you to Carolyn. You were my first "village member" and have been through it all with me from day one. If it weren't for you, I wouldn't have half the superpowers I do. And thank you to the "Bad News Bears" - Tina, Sarah, Danyel, Crystal, and Dawn. I am forever grateful for our gang and to have met each of you when I did. Without you, I wouldn't have found my long lost self.

Section 4

REMEMBERING WHO YOU WERE, CELEBRATING WHO YOU HAVE BECOME, AND BEING WHO YOU ARE

FEATURING
Naomi Haupt
Lila Beijer
Shannon-Lee Figsby
Candice Renee Blight
Sunit Suchdev

OPENING COMMENTARY BY
Sabrina Greer

I REMEMBER BEING IN LONDON after my big breakup, it was one of those *I'm single, heartbroken, and literally homeless so I need out* kinda trips. I was anxious and sad, and my best friend was living in Brixton. I tend to get a major travel bug when there's no reason to be in one place; nothing or nobody holding me down. I have always been referred to as a wanderer. One of my favorite quotes is by J. R. R. Tolkien, *"Not all those who wander are lost."* I have been to over two dozen countries and called half of them home but never felt "lost." I was just fortunate to have a career and a personality that supported this kind of freedom and flexibility. This time was different though. I needed my village, my girl; I needed someone to help me pick up the pieces of my broken heart and busted ego.

I didn't know why, but at the time, everywhere we looked, we saw babies. On the Tube, in coffee shops, even on pub patios. I was newly unattached and in London for seven consecutive sunny days (anyone who has ever been to the UK knows this is a big deal), but here I was, seeing babies at every turn rather than eligible bachelors. Every direction, little strollers were pushing around adorable accent possessors of the future. *Why is this happening?* You know when you're shopping for a specific car, and suddenly it's like everyone drives precisely that car? Make, model, and color, showing up everywhere. *Did I want a baby? Was this my notorious "ticking clock" I keep hearing about? Is this a sign or just a cruel joke? Was I with child? Could I be pregnant? I suppose mathematically, I could.* I peed on a stick that weekend, and the results were thankfully a definite negative. However, I later found out my bestie was, in fact, pregnant; they conceived that very weekend, with nothing but a wall between us (*thanks, guys*). My adorable little nephew is almost six-years-old now.

In less than six months, I spent five weeks in Peru (a trip that was initially planned with Mr. Unfaithful), a week in London, and a week in Bermuda. All of these trips served a purpose, a journey of self-discovery. I felt so misplaced after my breakup and didn't know who I was anymore; it was as though I had been stripped of my **identity** and my **future** all at once. I felt ripped off, like time was stolen from me; time I couldn't get back, precious moments just wasted. I spent months in this massive pity party state while repairing the damage. I needed to mourn this relationship, but more so the version of myself I had become around this person, I had to say goodbye to her because she was not the real me.

It's funny how sometimes it takes going as far away from what you know and what's comfortable, to remember who you are, at your core.

The moral of this story is that it didn't take long for me to find myself again. To find the girl I had always been. She showed up somewhere between a pregnancy test in the loo of a Brixton apartment and a six-day grueling hike through the Andes. You see, you cannot let someone else alter your being. Of course, people will change us; they make us stretch and grow. They teach us lessons and help us see different versions of ourselves (good or bad). I'm not suggesting closing yourself off to love, friendship, or opportunity, but you can't allow someone to change who you truly are; you must protect that with all you've got. This includes our children.

Inevitably motherhood changes us. We feel love and compassion like never before. We have new worries and fears that couldn't have existed without the presence of these little people. We learn new lessons every day; some small and some life-changing. It is very easy with all of this change and "new" to, somewhere along the way, forget who we were and who we are. It is not my academic degree or multiple certifications that accredits me to advise you here, it is my personal experiences of losing my true self. Mama to mama, woman to woman, trust me when I say, please hold on to her. Always treasure your core values. Remember the things that bring you joy and spark your flame, do those, often, like every day.

I met my hubby twenty-two days after I returned from Peru. *Twenty-two days.* I was ready, he was ready; we were ready to find each other. Right from the moment we first exchanged words, he made it crystal clear that he would never want someone to be something they were not. He came with massive baggage; I'm talking quadruple the size of my Peruvian travel pack. Although most relationships past middle school do come with a past. He had a six-year-old child, a similar half mangled heart, and a badly bruised ego, but I did not require he change any of it, nor did he pretend to be anyone but exactly who he is.

The authors in this section hit this message home. You are so much more than "just a mom," and if you are ever feeling any other way, I hope the chapters in this section provide you with the tools to rediscover what you need. Something I have found to be empowering and helpful is writing in my journal. Every day, write down five things you are grateful for, five things you love about yourself, and five things you want to accomplish. These do not need to be paragraph long and epic. *Today I am thankful for the clean air I have in my lungs* (grateful), *I love how my smile makes other people smile* (self-love), *I would like to take a walk in the fresh air today and smile at a stranger* (accomplishment). This simple daily commitment will fill your cup and remind you of **your** core values throughout the day. You need to be the best version of yourself, take care of yourself, love yourself, nourish yourself and **BE** yourself before you can effectively give anything back to your children or anyone else. This might be the most challenging undertaking in motherhood, period. We feel guilty, even selfish at times or like horrible mothers, but I sincerely believe this is the key to an empowered motherhood.

"Fill yourself up first and give from the overflow"
~ *Melissa Ambrosini.*

You've got this, Mama!

16

WHO WE WERE
AND WHO WE ARE

by Naomi Haupt

"You are beautiful. You are worthy. You are worth it."

Naomi Haupt

Naomi Haupt was born and raised in Colorado, U.S.A. She takes great interest in people and cultures and has been part of multiple outreach and learning opportunities around the world. An outdoors enthusiast, Naomi trained and worked as a backpacking guide in the Rocky Mountains. She is also an artist and musician and participates in various musical ensembles, planning to eventually write and record original music. Naomi has always loved writing and has published pieces in poetry, short fiction, and non-fiction. She graduated from Colorado State University in 2010 and married her husband, Charlton, in 2011. Naomi worked for a time as a teacher liaison, helping establish and write curriculum for energy conservation clubs in public schools before transitioning to staying home full time to raise her children.

Through her own experience as a mother and in talking to many other moms, Naomi gained a passion for helping moms to thrive amidst the challenges of raising small children. She founded The Moms' Happiness Project in 2017 to provide authentic, supportive community and practical strategies and tools for women in the thick of early motherhood.

Naomi is the author of *The Mom's Handbook to Happiness* and is working on upcoming publications and resources for mothers.

An advocate of women's health and Christian living, Naomi is also a speaker and loves to share about life, God's incredible love, and being a mom.

themomshappinessproject.com
ig: @momshappinessproject
fb: 4themoms

"For what you see and hear depends a good deal
on where you are standing…"
~ C.S. Lewis, The Magician's Nephew

I'D ALWAYS WANTED TO BE A MOM. Career goals were never a part of my daydreams of the future; I went to college, got a degree that I didn't plan on using much, but wanted to have as a "just-in-case." Just in case I didn't get married soon, just in case I needed to have my own income, just in case for some unexpected reason, it took awhile to have babies. Being a mom was my dream; my unadulterated dream where I was going to have eight perfect children and entirely love pregnancy, be beautifully empowered by childbirth, and enjoy every second of raising my sweet little ones.

Ah, naivety… all unicorns and roses.

There are a few memories from life so far that are forever imprinted on my brain. Three of those are discovering that each of my babies was growing inside of me. With our first, we found out in a Safeway parking lot. (See? Unicorns and roses). My husband and I were out of town visiting family; we had been trying for several months to get pregnant, and this was the day to check. The Day. That anticipated day after two weeks of waiting, hoping beyond hope that my dad-gum period would stay away and that I'd be able to see that second line show up on a pregnancy test. We stopped at Walgreens for a test, but not wanting to be too awkward and walk from the checkout stand directly to the bathroom with a pee stick in hand, I asked my husband to drive across the street to the Safeway. Heading inside alone, I made my way to the restroom, peed on the stick, forced myself not to check early while waiting for the allotted time, finally glanced down, and there on the test, plain as day, was one line.

sigh

One stupid line.

I almost chucked the test in the trash can, but knew my husband would want to see it too. So into my purse it went, and a good thing, because the first thing my husband said after I returned to the car and handed him the test, lamenting that it was negative and trying not to be too disappointed, was, "It's positive!"

"What?"

"It's positive. Look, it's right there."

Grabbing the test back, I looked again, more carefully this time, and sure enough, there it was. The second line. Faint (we compared it about fifty times to the little diagram in the pregnancy test instructions. *Is it close to picture number one? It says a faint line is still a positive. Is it like this picture? Does that even count as a line?*), but there. I was pregnant. One step closer to my daydream coming true.

Welp, that baby grew. We tracked every milestone, photographed every week's belly change, planned for me to quit my job, collected diapers, crib sheets, and tiny outfits… filled with that deep excitement of knowing something beautiful is coming; something wished for, something waited for.

I think it was about twelve hours into labor when reality began to infiltrate my fantasy of motherhood. By hour twenty, I was trying not to panic. By that final hour - hour twenty-three, I was reaching into depths of lingering strength I didn't even know existed.

Twenty-three hours of more pain than I would have thought possible. Running on next to no sleep, contractions ripping through hour after hour, pacing… trembling… puking… scraping every ounce of energy I could muster to push… *hard… harder… breathe…* grasp the oxygen mask and throw it aside… *push again…* blood vessels breaking… muscles straining… *push harder…* bellowing from the deepest recesses of all that I am… burning… tearing… birthing.

And in the midst of the most intense sense of relief that the ordeal is over, I'm handed a slippery, wailing, beautiful baby. He's mine. *How is this possible? What is this raw miracle? A person. A completely unique little person just came out of my body. He's mine... I'm his mother, and I can't comprehend this. I'm his mother... I'm a mom. That's who I am now.*

I don't know how to do this.

Oh, sweet mothers... how can we describe the weight and depth of motherhood? The deep internal battles that rage between intense love for our little ones and intense struggle over all that it takes to raise them? How do we describe the feeling of speaking gently to our screeching newborn and watching him calm at the sound of our voice, turning his delicate head to find the one his little heart loves? How do we speak of long nights spent in exhausting cycles of shallow sleep and nursing the baby, trying to keep depression at bay, wondering if we're actually cut out for this, staring at our tiny, beautiful child, wanting to sleep, wishing for morning, and dreading that night would come again? How do we describe the hair-tearing, face-palming, heart-squeezing days of toddlerhood? The strange concept of teeth-gritting frustration and unending adoration for this little person who drives us to the brink of insanity while still melting our hearts with bubbly laughs and light-filled smiles? How do we talk about seeing our young ones running around, knowing that within them is the power to both break our hearts and bring us profound joy? How do we describe the loneliness of being always with our children? The sameness of day after day that is both a frustrating monotony and peaceful simplicity? How do we describe the guilt, the anxiety, the mental weariness, the laughter, the satisfaction, the love? How do we paint the difficulty and beauty as one?

I've met and talked with a lot of moms over the last several years. The process of writing *The Mom's Handbook to Happiness* included surveying over nine hundred moms. Through interviews and surveys, we narrowed down the challenges of early motherhood to eight main battles. Of the eight battles, one that's surfaced again and again is the question of identity.

For the first three years or so of being a mom, I internally fought the reality of the sacrifice and constancy of motherhood. The arrival of our precious little boy had changed everything! (Funny how someone so small can do that). I thoroughly enjoyed the sweet times and deeply loved my son, but it seemed like a fire inside of me, part of who I am, was slowly dying. Activities my husband and I enjoyed prior to having kids such as backpacking, traveling, mountain climbing - became simple walks through the neighborhood and a game of Scrabble before we fell asleep. Dreams of extensive writing, music-playing, and adventuring were put on hold indefinitely. Everything about me and what I could do, it seemed, was changed by this role of being a mom, and that was a hard pill to swallow. Honestly, I felt guilty for struggling with it too, because after all, this is what I had dreamed about! I'd always wanted children, and while part of me was deeply satisfied in this new journey, another part of me bucked against the sacrifice required.

It took about three years of kicking against this reality to begin to understand a few things:

- Accept this for what it was… A season. Not my whole life, just a season.
- Realize the importance of nourishing my identity as a whole. Not just the "mom" part, but all of it.
- Recognize that nourishing identity has two sides – self-care and heart fires.

These three truths, precious mothers, can make a world of difference.

Just A Season

There's a story shared by a friend of mine, Abigail – a mom of three little boys now, the first two being twins, which beautifully encapsulates the freeing truth of seasons in life, particularly seasons in motherhood. I'll share it here in her words.

"Most of my memories of babyhood are wrapped up in remembering just having to walk outside while holding the twins because it was the only way I could get them not to cry. It honestly was one of the hardest, most terrible times of my life. My mom told me (and she's taken care of many, many babies), that they were the absolute fussiest babies that she'd ever seen, and that would have even been true if there was just one of them, but there were two! And they were equally fussy! In Arkansas, it stays relatively hot from the end of April until the beginning of October. The boys were born in February but didn't really "wake up" until around the beginning of April because of being pree-mies. I remember thinking that summer would never end. I now refer to that time as "baby purgatory." They hated being inside, they hated the stroller, they hated being in the car, they hated being in bouncers. When they were about seven months old, they would tolerate being in an exersaucer for about fifteen minutes, twice a day, and they were willing to play on the floor sitting (they didn't sit on their own until they were eight months old) for about five minutes, twice a day. All the rest of the time, I was carrying both of them (not in a wrap, mind you, in my arms, because most of the time, wraps were a no-go) facing outward while I walked. They would not sit on my hips while I held them. I had to walk (I couldn't sit, or they would cry), outside. All day. Every single damn day. Until they were ten months old. When they started crawling, it was like a switch flipped, and suddenly they were just happy, sweet babies and infinitely, less high maintenance.

There were times when I'd be walking around the front yard and start thinking, *I can't do this anymore, I just can't. I can't live this way, what am I going to do?* Sometimes I'd just have to lay them down even though they were screaming, and walk away for a few minutes, but most of the time, I'd just tell myself, this is just a season. This is just one season out of their whole lives, and it's going to pass. Children grow; it's basically their job. It's what they do. They will not be five-years-old wanting me to carry them around the yard; this is going to get better. This is JUST. ONE. SEASON. And for one season, you can do this."

Just a season. Not our whole lives, just a season. And while the sacrifice is real, oh my goodness, the beauty is real too. Does motherhood change things? Ohhh yes. In good ways and hard ways. Mothering little ones is all-consuming in some regards, but it will not be this way forever. One day, there will be more time and less exhaustion. One day, our babies will no longer be babies. One day, there will be no more butts to wipe, pacifiers to find, or cries to calm in the middle of the night. One day, our kiddos will demand far less of us. From what I've heard, it's a bittersweet shift.

I've learned (and am still learning as a mom of three littles now) to enjoy being so needed, to accept and appreciate the simplicity of this season, and to focus on the sweetness rather than what I cannot do. This time will change, and the next season will have its own set of joys and hardships.

Nourishing Identity

Amidst the reality of seasons, there's also the reality of you. You as a whole, not just as a mom. It can be so easy to let ourselves slip down to the bottom of the priority list in the name of "caring for the family." However, while sacrifice and selflessness certainly are the core of many parts of mothering, we don't do ourselves, our marriage, or our children any favors by being completely overtaken by the role of "mom."

I know one mom who is now in her fifties. Her first babies, twins, came when she was twenty-one years old and a third child only fourteen months later. For nineteen years, she wrapped herself up entirely in being their mother. Diapers, laundry, meals, wrangling kiddos, loving them, protecting them... band-aids, doctor visits, sick days, school, sports, conversations, discipline, pride, high school graduation... and then they left the house. Within a year, all three of them were off on their own. This woman was lost. Devastated. She was a wonderful mom, but when the day-to-day of that role ceased, she literally didn't know what to do with herself and has struggled deeply ever since – not sure of who she is, not sure what her role in life looks like now, not sure if she is still important.

In the years of learning to accept the day-to-day and long-term changes that came along with our precious newborn boy, I also began to realize something else... I am still me. Parts of me have changed, grown, been refined. What I can do and cannot do in any given season will change, will ebb and flow, will have to shift and make room, and sometimes be given up altogether, but I am still me. I am a mom. I am also a wife, a sister, a daughter, a friend, a musician, a writer, an artist, an outdoors-lover, an adventurer, etc. I am beautiful. I am important. I am worthy. Not just because I'm a mom, but because I'm a woman and a human being.

You, sweet mother, are beautiful. You are important. You are worthy. Your identity is not defined by your role as a mom. It's okay, and it's good, to nourish other parts of who you are.

Self-Care And Heart Fires

Nourishing identity is all well and good in theory, but what does it practically look like in our day-to-day? After all, the days are more than full and often unpredictable, which is why taking care of ourselves can so easily be pushed to the back burner.

When it comes to keeping your identity alive, it ultimately boils down to two categories that are both extremely important. The first is self-care. Take care of yourself. A lot of self-care simply means personal hygiene, but let's be honest, when you have little tykes, basic personal hygiene isn't always the top priority. Showers are often crammed into a few minutes between nap times, getting dressed means throwing a t-shirt on with a pair of sweats, and "brushing" is a choice between your hair or teeth, whichever seems more important at the time. Working out? Ha! That takes time. And time is not exactly in abundance. *Do I really want to spend a precious half hour of the day tiring myself out? Isn't that what I do the rest of the time anyway in a different form? Does carrying a baby in a car seat around constitute as lifting weights?* All valid questions, those things are heavy!

Seriously though, it's super important to take care of yourself. Get some exercise. Eat good food. Take a shower. Drink lots of water. Take care of your body so that you can be healthy, present, and feel like a normal human being. Research suggests that our physical health and mental health are very much intertwined.[7] Taking care of your physical health has a profound impact on your self-esteem and overall ability to handle each day's challenges, and Lord knows that life raising little ones is full of those!

Besides basic health and hygiene, it's also important to do things that make you feel good about yourself. Wear clothes that you like and make you feel happy about the way you look. Paint your nails. Get a fresh haircut. Maybe buy a new outfit once in a while (especially after months on end of wearing maternity clothes!). Different personalities will obviously vary in what falls into this realm of self-care. However, the

7   Young, Joel (2014, October 2). *9 Lifestyle Factors That Can Affect Your Mental Health.* Retrieved from www.psychologytoday.com/blog/when-your-adult-child-breaks-your-heart/201410/9-lifestyle-factors-can-affect-your-mental

point is, you need to still feel like a strong, healthy, confident woman both physically and mentally to help you remember that you are, in fact, a strong, healthy, confident woman who is both a wonderful mother and a valuable person with much to offer the world.

Granted, off days happen. Spit up and poop are part of life. An awfully big part, some days. Both of my boys were huge spitter-uppers. I don't know how many times my entire shirt front was completely soaked and smelled terrible. Some days you just hit the ground running and are glad everyone's still alive at the end of it. So regardless of poop, puke, and other such explosive possibilities, the point is to make sure you prioritize your own body and health in your day-to-day. It doesn't have to be complicated or take a lot of time, but it shouldn't be neglected entirely.

The other category in the identity matter is that of the heart fires. Keep your dreams! They are part of you. A very important part that doesn't need to die just because you're raising children. Now, of course, some things will change. I've finally accepted the reality that I can't do everything I ever want to do in life, but I can do some. What excites you? What's something you've always wanted to accomplish? What's something you just enjoy? Maybe you're an artist. Maybe a musician. Maybe a nurse. Maybe a businesswoman. Maybe a writer. Maybe a pastry chef. Maybe you love to garden, or bird watch, or run marathons. Keep those things alive, in some respect or another. It doesn't have to be a roaring fire, but it can at least be a pile of embers. This doesn't have to be a daily, or even necessarily, a weekly occurrence; it will naturally ebb and flow, but do *something*. Whatever it may be for you, the key is to keep up, however small the amount may be, with something or things you enjoy.

Now there is, of course, the time factor. Realistically, caring for little ones takes most of the day and sometimes most of the night. So how does this look practically? Depending on what you're doing, it may require finding a part-time childcare solution. If it can be a good situation that gives you the pieces of time you need, it's totally worth it. Grandparents, aunts, and uncles can come in very handy here. Otherwise, make the most of nap times and bedtimes. Honestly, this is when almost all of my non-child-care related activities take place. Our older two no longer take naps most days, so we kept it as "rest time" for them (i.e., they look at books, color, watch a movie, play in the basement, etc. on their own while the baby is sleeping). This is my main avenue of production. Once or twice a week, I'll also utilize time after the kiddos are in bed. My husband and I make Monday night a time to work on projects we enjoy and / or need to finish. With the expectation set for that to be a "work evening," I can look forward to having time set aside for non-kid stuff and still know we'll have time to spend together on the other evenings.

Again, everyone's situation is different, but as long as we're finding some way or ways to nourish our identity apart from motherhood, both our families and we will be better off for it. After all, our children watch what we do. When they see us thriving, they will learn to thrive. They will learn our way of living. They will learn joy. They will learn sacrifice. They will learn priorities. They will learn to care for both themselves and others. They will learn to enjoy something for the sake of enjoyment, for the sake of beauty.

So hang in there, Mama! This motherhood thing is crazy hard and crazy beautiful, all at the same time. I still have off days; that's part of life, part of living. It's okay to struggle. Having hard days is okay. It's okay to want time to yourself sometimes. It's okay to roll your eyes when you finally get back to your coffee, and it's cold. It's okay to work on a project, keep a job, go to the gym, do push-ups in your living room when a gym is out of the question. It's okay to shut your door and take deep breaths. It's okay to cry. It's okay to learn to like yourself again. You are beautiful. You are worthy. You are worth it.

May you know how incredibly valuable you really are, precious mother, and may you be infinitely blessed as you journey on.

~ To my babies... you are more precious to me than you will ever know. And to Charlton... thank you for your strong arms and steady spirit, for being right there with me. I love doing this life with you!

17

MORE THAN
JUST A "MOM"

by Lila Beijer

"The magic of every day comes with personally inspired action." xoxo

Lila Beijer

Lila lives each day fueled by her desire to live an extraordinary life. A traveler at heart, her adventures began by sailing around the world to exotic destinations for six years which was where she met her husband. A devoted mother to three incredible boys, Lila shows her children what living gratefully and with intention looks like. Lila's entrepreneurial spirit had her start up a business with a health and wellness company called Arbonne International, which has become so much more than a business; a way to maintain a healthy lifestyle. This allows her to work on her terms and use her free time to pursue her passions. Photography was one that excited her, and now alongside Arbonne, is at the forefront of her professional life. She dabbles in workouts and trading cryptocurrency to keep things interesting and diverse. She leads with a passionate heart and is an aspiring philanthropist. When she's not out enjoying life with her loved ones, she retreats to her cozy bed that doubles as an office. Often planning for great adventures... Lila is described as a unicorn with rainbow coloured glasses and a fiery spirit.

Side note: She likes to be surprised and to surprise others.

www.lilabeijer.arbonne.com
ig: @LilasLens

"As unique as we all are, an awful lot of us want the same things.
We want to shake up our current less-than-fulfilling lives.
We want to be happier, more loving, forgiving and connected
with the people around us."
~ Brené Brown

I N WHAT I OFTEN REFER to as my previous life, you know the one, pre-babies, where I lived one heck of an exciting and unpredictable life. Waking up in different countries every day, secluded islands and different beaches, every day a party! I was an officer on a six-star cruise line for years. I wore pretty gowns and ate the best foods from around the world. I fell in love - twice! I made more money than I could keep track of and lived a life I would envy if it were not my own!

Fast forward to 2012, I am a mom to two amazing and healthy boys, a wife, and a proud, hard-working woman in the corporate world. We had a great routine - our little family had it all figured out.

Who Me? Couldn't Be!

Then came the day I found out I was pregnant with my third child. Boy, was it a scary one! After three different pregnancy tests confirmed, the horror of it all set in. This has to be the worst timing ever! The news came the very same week I had finished with diaper changes after four straight years! The nausea set in hard, doctor's appointments were booked with blood tests, and an ultrasound appointment to date the pregnancy.

Then it came, the doctor's call. She said, "The pregnancy is not viable. I'm sorry. Wait for a miscarriage, and if it doesn't happen in ten days, we will proceed with a D&C (Dilation and curettage, essentially removing the contents from the uterus)." The roller coaster of emotion I experienced was difficult, to say the least. A bit of relief mixed with a ton of guilt. I decided to go see someone who allowed me to have an emotional release of acceptance and a sort of ceremonial goodbye with this "non-viable" fetus. It was therapeutic, and I felt ready (as ready as one can be) to miscarry.

Day eleven - nothing had happened yet. And so we were going for the removal of this fetus when a doctor from the genetics department ran some tests and asked us to give him an hour. My husband and I walked through the hospital gardens, taking in its beauty, emotionally prepared for this and reminded ourselves how fortunate we were that we had two wonderful, healthy boys and that was really all we ever wanted anyway.

The test results were in, and the doctor, very matter of factly says, "I have no idea why your doctor believed this pregnancy to be non-viable - EVERYTHING LOOKS PERFECTLY NORMAL!" Now, he didn't yell, but that is how it sounded to me and continued to for a few minutes. I sat there like a deer in headlights as I allowed this shocking statement to circle around my brain.

Here We Go Again!

This is the moment my life flipped upside down. We had to start again. The pregnancy came with additional ultrasounds to make sure there were no hidden surprises that had initially alerted my family doctor. Seven months pregnant with weekly ultrasounds of me joking, "Ten fingers, ten toes?" and the same response, "All looks great," stopped. They told me to just enjoy the next couple of months as a family of four. Perfect!

We decided to have a c-section, for several reasons, and most importantly for me to have my tubes cauterized - no more little miracles were going to be coming out of me! It's hard enough to get dinner reservations for five, so no thank you!

Finally, it was D-day, and we were all ready (as ready as a woman can be) for this, but nothing truly prepares you for this moment. The moment the baby comes out and the doctor comes right up to your face and says, "Something's wrong." The shock set in, the room went silent, and I mean, dead silent. I couldn't hear my baby, nor the nurses, or doctors. Then came the commanding voice of my husband yelling, "Give me the baby!" He brought our baby boy so close to my face and said, "He's perfect!" The little one was crying, and noise flooded back into the room. The doctor talked to me, but I couldn't hear a word she was saying to me. I felt a mix of relief knowing that our baby was fine and was slowly recovering from the shock of her words.

The next thing I recall is being in recovery, nursing our little boy, and not at all comprehending why he has eleven fingers. My thoughts were running wild, because of hormones, mixed with Gravol and whatever else they gave me to calm me down. *What is wrong with him? What did I do? What did I eat? The doctor said something's wrong, is it something else as well? Is he damaged?*

Over the next three days, I could not manage to look at my baby properly. My husband and I could not agree on a name. I was frustrated and fought with him. He could not understand my shame in all of this. He kept joking in the best way he knew how to try to make me laugh and would say, better eleven than nine. I hated him then and wanted to be alone in my sadness. I felt defeated and so out of control.

We finally agreed on the name Jonah. Jonah who changed everything. Jonah who as it turns out only had one kidney, Jonah who needed to be taken to genetics every few weeks so they could see if anything else was wrong. Jonah, Jonah, Jonah! I felt like I was not able to give enough attention to my four-year-old and three-year-old, and I certainly wasn't taking care of myself. The stress was too much for my husband and I, and the arguing was constant. Lucky for him, he's a bartender, out for the evening and most of the night, and asleep most of the day. We decided I would not go back to work, and now this was all on me.

Why did this have to happen to us? There were even the occasional days I would feel so defeated, and Jonah was already a year old, I would call my sister and say, "I'm not sure I even love him. Things were going so well before Jonah. I'm exhausted!" Then after those words came out, I would scoop him up, hold him and kiss him, and whisper to him how much I love him. I knew even then that I did, I simply felt defeated. We are often told that when we have a child, our love for them will be instantaneous and unconditional. I knew my love was real, but it didn't feel right that I was questioning it. *What was wrong with me?*

Wine? Food? Pick Your Poison!

I had just stopped breastfeeding, and I felt lost. *What was my purpose now?* I loved my boys, and sometimes I even loved my husband. When the boys were sleeping and I was alone, I started to eat anything and everything. Some people choose wine, anything that "takes the edge off." I would eat until I no longer felt overwhelmed. I would eat to the point of not thinking of all the moms I knew, who seemed to have their shit together and were becoming everything they set out to be as mothers and working women. Comparing my life to others was one of my many triggers. Eating was such a relief. It brought me joy; it was my savior. I could take on the world, and no one even knew. The calories didn't matter because no one knew I was eating. It all made perfect sense to me. I felt like a magical unicorn that had her shit together, and I was unstoppable! The high was quick and powerful while the low was soul-sucking and felt like a punch in the gut. Then I was numb from it all.

I became as sad as I was full; I felt uncomfortable and ashamed of myself, and through tears, I made myself sick. *Get it out of me as fast as possible - I feel gross and I hate myself. How could I be a mom and be behaving like a teenage girl with body image issues? That's not who I am, is it?*

This continued for some time on and off. Nobody knew this was my reality. I enrolled the kids in before and after school programs, which meant I had a few extra hours to be irresponsible and selfish. Jonah was already three-years-old, and life was flying by. I sailed through the next year and a half, distracting myself with lunches with friends (lunches that I couldn't keep down), with shopping I couldn't afford, and ordering takeout at night. I was falling down a rabbit hole of self-destruction that I could not stop myself from. I was ashamed. And considering the stigma surrounding bulimia, this was not something I could ever share with anyone. *How had this become my life?*

"We cannot selectively numb emotions, when we numb the painful emotions, we also numb the positive emotions." ~ Brené Brown

Taking Control Of My Mind

It was time for a healthy distraction. I decided to focus on my home-based business. I started this business opportunity a few weeks before I took that life-changing pregnancy test, but with all the chaos that had ensued, my business did not get the attention it deserved. This new focus was going to force me out of my negative spiral. Being in the social networking industry, it forced me to get out and be social! This became a lifeline for me. A reminder that I was more than just a mom!

It became my golden chance to surround myself with inspiring people whose goal in life was to see others succeed. Success in this industry had so much to do with personal growth. Learning to live the life of our dreams by taking small, consistent, and daily actions towards those goals. My business partner linked arms with me and showed me how becoming the best version of myself in every aspect of life is what it would take for me to achieve the success I desired. I went to meetings, read personal development books, and followed a system that, I saw, worked for so many. The evidence of success was all around me. I found myself feeling happier than I had felt in a long time. There is nothing like placing yourself amongst happy, inspired people to put you on a temporary high.

I read this quote by Gabrielle Bernstein, *"So much of our suffering was based on projecting out what we don't want to feel. Acknowledging and honoring my wounds is the simplest way to feel better about myself and heal."*

Then, a realization set in. As my kids grew and evolved, I needed to do so as well. This is the evolution of parenting. Today, I am not stuck, I have everything it takes to become the best version of myself. I remember the times I was incredibly proud of myself. If I was enough once, I know I could be again. It was time to stop looking to outside sources for inspiration and start creating and finding inspiration within.

I Can Breathe Again

I began a bucket list project. A movement that would force me to put one foot in front of the other in the direction of my personally inspired life. I was thirty-seven-years-old, and so I set a goal to do thirty-seven things to be completed by year-end. I created a list of things I could get excited about, some would be small, like trying out a hot yoga class, and some would be more exciting like taking a photography class. That simple item to check off my list drove me to purchase a camera and by the end of that year become a paid lifestyle photographer. I would say YES to as many things as I could (that included crashing a wedding with my girlfriends! Eek!) and see what happened when I focused my attention on the things I want. I was all for messing up and not worrying about being perfect, and just going for things while surrendering to possibility.

I knew for certain that in order for me to truly live my best life, I needed to spend more time with my best boys. I realized that I actually love my role as a mother, so I immediately decided to take them out of the after-school program and spent time every day connecting with them, cuddling them, playing board games, and laughing a ton! I focused on each of them actively, almost feeling like I was making up for lost time. A time where I had drowned out their noise. Now loving all (well, almost all) of their craziness, I even shared with them my bucket list ideas. My eldest, who was eight-years-old at the time, was so inspired he created one of his own! Who knew my life could take such an inspired turn from one simple bucket list and saying yes to new experiences?

In Hindsight

Jonah spent so many days home with his dad, while I went out and tried to escape my reality. Grandparents were present and always full of love and support whenever I needed. I have the warmest friends a girl can ask for, whom I know would have listened without judgment, and the best sister (although she lives in a different time zone) who I can call anytime, day or night. I simply wasn't seeing things clearly. My emotions were controlling me and I felt lost for years. I have learned that hiding does not serve me. Communicating is vital. They say it takes a village. Well, I had my village, I just didn't know how to use it.

"Vulnerability sounds like truth and feels like courage. Truth and courage aren't always comfortable, but they're never weakness."
~ Brené Brown

Power Reclaimed

Today, I feel powerful. Life still has its messy moments, but of this I am confident - I am an amazing mother. I love my three boys and their different, wonderful personalities. I treasure my time with them, and without them. I have learned that it excites me to live a passionate life, full of new experiences, and that I want my sons to see what a mother and woman can be. All of my experiences and the lessons I have learned are what allow me to be the best version of myself and show my kids what living an authentic and inspired life looks like. A new list is being drawn up for the year ahead, and I'm excited to become the mother and woman I will grow into.

I am proud of the mother I am, and am excited by the woman I am becoming. I am grateful for the healing I have done and the life I am building for us. If you feel like you have lost yourself on this journey through motherhood, like I did, I encourage you to engage your village. You are not alone, Mama, and believe me when I say, if I've got this, you've got this!

~ Everyday is better than the last because of you three, my dear Jonah, Matthew, and Noah. Thank you for your gifts of laughter and love that inspire me to keep on growing.

18
CHARTING THE SEAS OF MOTHERHOOD

by Candice Renee Blight

"*Motherhood is about charting your own course and accepting that love is all you need*"

Candice Renee Blight

Born and raised in Vancouver, Canada, Candice is a passionate globetrotter, hobby photographer, and a true foodie! Notoriously adventurous, she always knew she'd live a life she loved and would never settle for less. As a young girl, she loved to be with people and was a passionate performer. Her tenacity and strong will would turn out to be her greatest strength. She pursued her love of adventure by moving to Florida for a year, working as a Canadian Ambassador at Walt Disney World's Epcot. She attended college and university, dabbling in the Restaurant business and Vancouver film industry. Rather than pursuing acting, she followed her deepest love of travel and took on a life at sea working on Celebrity, Norwegian, and Disney Cruise Lines, where she met her husband.

A master of many things, Candice has been a successful art auctioneer, restaurant manager, and real estate agent, but her favourite career came as a luxury brand consultant promoting shopping in exotic destinations. Known as one of the best in the business, Candice held presentations for thousands, and hosted onboard TV shows. Through cruising, backpacking, and simply hopping on the next plane, she has travelled to all continents except Antarctica, but it's on her list. Currently Candice pursues a busy West Coast life with her husband and baby boy, Hudson. She loves running, brunching, and writing for her travel and mommy blog. Extremely caring, organized, and a born leader, she's forever looking at the glass half full! This mama just loves life.

www.thismamaloveslife.com
candice@thismamaloveslife.com
ig: @thismamaloveslife
fb: thismamaloveslife
p: Thismamaloveslife | t: @candilane

"Everything has changed and yet, I'm more me than I have ever been."
~ Iain Thomas

I ALWAYS KNEW I WANTED TO BE A MOTHER. From a young age, I had it all carefully planned out. At age twenty-one, I was going to marry an insanely good looking and wealthy young man. Then at age twenty-three, this "prince charming" and I would give birth to a baby girl, "our little princess." We would live happily ever after, of course, and travel the world in style while doing it! Well, let's just say, I got the traveling the world part out of the way, married Mark, "MY" prince charming (who I find incredibly handsome) at age thirty, and gave birth to a beautiful little boy (*not* the girl I was expecting) a few years later. Life doesn't always turn out exactly how you dream it will as a ten-year-old girl, but I think I got pretty darn close. I like to call it my very own fairytale.

Pregnant At Sea

Working for the cruise lines, I've traveled to more countries than I can keep track of. I must have seen at least forty countries in the span of five years. When I met my husband, we shared this undying enthusiasm for adventure. On our first date, we rented a motorbike and ate gyros on a hilltop overlooking the sea in Santorini. Being in a new port every day, we fell in love while wandering around small fishing villages, tasting the local specialties, and photographing every picturesque moment! In the evenings and most nights, we would dine like the passengers, sometimes even with the passengers, discussing travel and adding exotic places to our bucket lists. We worked sometimes of course, but when I look back on the past decade, the life I was living was straight out of travel and leisure magazine. For our holidays, instead of sitting at home, we booked more vacations, but not cruise vacations - we went backpacking around South America, hiking to Machu Picchu in Peru, and visited Iguazu Falls in Brazil. We went on an incredible safari in Africa, visited the local schools in Tanzania, and explored the Tanzanite mine. One of our last trips was a romantic stay in Northern Italy. We stayed in a village on Lake Como down the street from George Clooney's villa and visited Bellagio and Verona. I was getting used to the life of a traveling nomad; nothing was tying us down or holding us back. If we hadn't gotten pregnant when we did, we probably wouldn't have stopped, and maybe, we never would have stopped.

I found out I was pregnant somewhere between Jamaica and The Bahamas. Having a slight suspicion that I could be, I had picked up a test from a drugstore in port the week before. While at sea, I sat on the toilet in our tiny officer's cabin onboard the Disney Fantasy. I could feel the swaying of the ship as I counted the seconds until those two faint pink lines appeared. I glared at it and shakily called for my husband. We hadn't exactly planned this (we weren't ready to give up our glamorous and unpredictable life), but with a smile on both our faces, we decided we would be okay. Something we had been putting off until who knows when, it was time for the next chapter of our lives to begin. The next morning, I took the elevator down to B deck where the cruise ship doctor was and spilled my news. I wasn't sure if I was allowed to be pregnant while working on a cruise ship. *Could I even get an ultrasound? What about Zika?* I had kept hearing about it all over the news, and it sounded frightening. Once I was back in my cabin, I went online and ordered all the pregnancy books I could find. I had an upcoming appointment in Grand Cayman for an ultrasound which would date the pregnancy, and I would be picking up prenatal vitamins next chance I got. I would spend my entire first trimester on a cruise ship. Luckily I never had to suffer morning sickness, and perhaps I have my sturdy sea legs to thank for this.

Merchants And Mosquitos

We had nine weeks left on our contract sailing in the Caribbean when we found out I was pregnant. During this time, a virus called Zika was prevalent in the region and could be transferred to a person via a simple mosquito bite. This virus is especially dangerous for pregnant women with the highest risk to a growing fetus. Babies were being born with unusually small heads (microcephaly) and other congenital abnormalities when born to infected mothers. Although not a risk for the majority of the population, pregnant women were warned not to travel to these regions, which was exactly what I was doing on a weekly basis.

I should mention that our job onboard consisted of going into the ports and meeting with merchants each day, and although I was "with child," there was still work to be done. We were independent contractors, and to make our targets, we usually needed to be the first people off in the morning and the last people back onboard. To protect myself, I was covered from head to toe in light-colored clothing (even though it was scorching hot outside and I just wanted to be in a bathing suit). I was re-applying deet to my clothes consistently and constantly watching my back. Really, I was watching my whole body from head to toe and freaking out! I'll never forget being inside a store in St. Thomas and feeling like I was surrounded by Zika infected mosquitoes. I remember thinking I was more afraid of these tiny disease-carrying insects than man-eating great white sharks! I'm not sure if my mind was playing tricks on me, but I constantly heard them buzzing in my ear. After having a breakdown in the middle of Charlotte Amalie in the US Virgin Islands, Mark and I both agreed I would stay onboard as much as possible. So the days we went to the ports where they had recent cases, that's precisely what I did. I literally felt confined to my cabin on some days. I had, what is known as, cabin fever: A type of hysteria brought on by spending too much time indoors. Directly descended from long-haul journeys where you are stuck in cramped conditions for too damn long! Okay it wasn't actually that bad, I mean we were living on a 5-star Disney cruise ship.

The hardest part was that we weren't telling anyone I was pregnant yet. Our co-workers and business contacts had no idea of our expanding situation. I didn't want to risk my job, but I knew the most important thing was the little person growing inside me. People kept making comments about Zika saying, "Well at least, you're not pregnant," or "You're not pregnant, are you?" I couldn't sleep some nights, especially after seeing the images on the news of these poor, deformed children, and just yearned to get home to safety.

We were counting down the weeks until this contract finished. I literally jumped off the ship on that final day, and we flew from Florida to London and drove to Mark's parents' home in South Devon. We couldn't wait to tell his family the news, but I longed to get home to my family doctor to ensure everything was okay.

The first week of October, we were finally home in Vancouver. Listening to my baby's heartbeat was surreal, and definitely the most beautiful sound I had ever heard. My doctor got me in to see the specialist right away and scheduled an ultrasound. When I saw our baby's body moving on the screen, I was filled with relief. With tears welling up in my eyes, I asked the technician if the head was of normal size and she replied, "Absolutely." I could finally sleep at night. I received my blood test results a few days later which confirmed I hadn't contracted Zika while in the Caribbean.

Labor Of Love

I started going to prenatal yoga once a week. I loved connecting with my belly and baby and hoped it would better prepare me for birth. Going to yoga taught me to want an all natural birth, and was intent on not having a c-section; something almost all of my friends have needed for one reason or another. I was given a book by my yoga instructor called, *Birthing from Within.* She also spoke a lot about "home birthing," and although I was definitely going to the hospital, I had convinced myself I didn't want any drugs, mostly because I was told they increase your chances of needing a cesarean. Also, I wanted to hold and nurse my baby immediately after delivering without the long and limiting recovery time.

I literally labored at home for days, and once finally admitted to the hospital, I hadn't slept in three nights. Although exhausted, I turned down the epidural when it was offered and continued to brave the pain. I had contractions constantly, but my cervix was dilating way too slowly. Eventually, the doctor sat us down and started talking about labor intervention and said the word I was dreading - Pitocin. I feared that this was going to lead to a c-section, or baby's heart rate being affected, both of which were things I wanted to avoid. The major concern was my uterus becoming tired, which could result in severe complications and internal bleeding. Well, I was definitely VERY TIRED, my entire body felt fatigued.

At this point, I just wanted my baby out safely. My doctor explained that the best chance of birthing this baby vaginally and safely would be augmenting the labor with Pitocin and receiving the dreaded epidural. This was definitely NOT a part of my birth plan, but I hesitantly agreed. I needed rest if I wanted to be able to push this baby out physically.

When the anesthesiologist arrived, he asked me if I was aware of all the risks involved and volunteered to explain them. *UM… No thank you.* Of course, I didn't want to listen to his "laundry list" of all the risks including brain damage, paralysis, and death! I listened very closely to every instruction given and tried to stay as still as possible as he stuck the humongous needle in my back. I hated the feeling of having these drugs pumped into me, and I felt like a "numb slug" lying there confined to the hospital bed! The silver lining was I was finally able to REST! They started to administer the Pitocin, and I rested without pain for at least two hours. By the grace of God, it worked, and soon I was dilated nine and a half centimeters wide, ready to go! They stopped the Pitocin, the epidural wore off, and I began pushing. I could feel everything including the "Ring of Fire," but by this time, I had my stamina and energy back. Through-out the pain, all I could think about was how each push was getting me closer to meeting my little guy! I knew the doctor could have easily made a little "snip," and he would have been out, but I was determined to do it on my own without tearing (if at all possible). Well, it was possible, and that final push was a feeling I will never forget, a completely amazing sensation as I felt and watched our beautiful baby, Hudson, being born. I was so grateful to my doctor who coached me so well, and the support I had from my loving hubby and mother. Thank goodness I had them, and thank goodness they had each other. Although my birth plan went out the window (which I knew they usually do), it couldn't have gone any better! I learned to have an open mind at times like these. I didn't have my completely natural birth experience that I had hoped for, but it really didn't matter once I was holding my baby in my arms. In fact, the next time I might just ask for that giant needle!

The Scary Phone Call

When Hudson was four days old, I received a call from my doctor's of-fice. Not the doctor who delivered Hudson, or my family doctor, but a doctor who was filling in. She told me they had received the results from the Hospital Newborn Screening and that my son had tested positive for a Rare Genetic Metabolic Disorder called "VLCAD." She tried to pronounce each word and explain the meaning of it, but by this time, the room was already spinning, and I slumped to the floor.

I cannot explain how scary it was to have someone tell you there is something wrong with your child. My newborn baby, who I loved more than anything in the world, my baby who was absolutely perfect in my eyes. The doctor on the phone continued to tell me that they would be doing further testing to confirm, as this particular disorder had a high level of false positives, and his markers were not "sky high." She said that maybe it wasn't a good idea to "google" the disorder until we spoke to the experts from Children's Hospital. I shakily hung up the phone and stared at my seemingly perfect baby boy. Surely, this was a mistake. Of course, I immediately "googled" it and skimmed over a sentence that made my heart skip a beat. "If untreated, VLCAD can cause brain damage and even death." *Did I just read death?*

Luckily, my mom was over at the time, as Mark was back at work. Mothers always know the right things to say. She put aside her own fear and uncertainty to calm me down and reassure me. I was so exhausted; I just wanted to fall asleep and wake up thinking this was just a bad dream. The next morning, Children's Hospital called, and Mark and I brought Hudson in that very day for blood tests. The doctor explained to us that our baby looked very healthy and possibly had a mild form of the disorder or was just an unaffected carrier. VLCAD is a fatty acid oxidation disorder, which means one cannot properly break down fat from either the food they eat or from fat stored in their bodies. They sent us home with an emergency letter (just in case) and told me to make sure Hudson didn't go more than three hours without feeding. For almost a month, we waited for the results to come back, hoping and praying that they would come back negative. As I was exclusively nursing, I set my alarm clock for both day and night to ensure he was consistently fed, and never slept for too long.

One day we were on the way to Children's Hospital, for a scheduled appointment with the cardiologist for Hudson, when the metabolic doctor called to tell us that he didn't have VLCAD. We still had the echocardiogram done and were even happier when we were told his heart was normal and everything looked great. Every time they checked Hudson, he presented as a happy, healthy, beautiful baby, but they wanted to do more blood tests to find out what was causing these abnormal results. A few weeks later we were told he had a mild form of another genetic metabolic disorder called Multiple acyl-CoA dehydrogenase deficiency (MADD). Children with MADD usually are very sick and have visible external abnormalities, but Hudson hadn't had any symptoms to date, and he looked just fine. Just when I thought our worries were over, my heart sank again. There was so much unknown. They sent us home with a prescription for Riboflavin which we were to administer twice a day with a syringe. Riboflavin is a vitamin complex which is meant to treat the disorder, but because Hudson had no symptoms, we were technically trying to treat his numbers, and the doctors said nothing changed on his charts anyways. So, as challenging as it was, for about a month, we gave him this sweet neon-orange-colored medicine, before he even tasted pureed food.

My baby has had more blood tests than I've probably had in my entire life, but at least the specialists are proactive, and if we end up having to deal with a late-onset form of MADD, then we will deal with it every way we can. If this happens, we may have to follow a low-fat, low-protein, high-carbohydrate diet, and avoid any fasting periods. There are adult symptoms that we definitely never want our son to experience, so we will take this in stride, and just be grateful, as it could be much worse. It's so unusual that both my husband and I carry this exact gene variant that they still have very little information about. I'm just thankful everyday that Hudson is a healthy and happy baby boy.

From Travel And Leisure To SAHM

Undeniably life changes, and my life has seen BIG changes since I've become a mother. Our small apartment has been taken over by play mats, jolly jumpers, and exersaucers. My husband has gone to working a regular day job, and I have been staying at home trying to balance mom life and raising my little human in the best way I know how. I believe everything happens for a reason, and I was meant to be a mama. I thought my travel days were numbered once we had a baby, but Hudson already has more stamps in his passport than most middle-aged people. Traveling with an infant was easier than I thought it would be, it just took a little planning. At three months, we took him to England, Spain, then across Canada to cottage country to spend a week at the lake with our family. At nine months, we took a fifteen plus hour flight to Australia where we spent Christmas in Sydney's Northern Beaches! I can't wait to show him the world and share my passion for travel with him. It hasn't been easy adjusting to a life on land, but waking up each day and holding my baby boy in my arms is the best feeling in the world, and if I had to choose, I wouldn't trade it to visit forty more countries!

Life Travels On

With literally a million sources telling you what works, I learned that I needed to discover for myself what works best. My journey into motherhood was about charting my own course, making my own decisions, and in the end, accepting the fact that love is really all you need. We've had scary moments and times where we've struggled, but each experience has made us stronger. Although I have gone from a busy travel lifestyle and career to being a stay at home mom, I wouldn't change a thing. Trading those sea legs and suitcases for strollers and SUVs is one of my biggest life achievements. I plan on continuing to travel the world with my little family, and one day even take Hudson on a magical Disney Cruise. Luckily, I've saved my favorite suitcase to do so.

"The world is a book, and those who do not travel read only a page."
~ Saint Augustine

~ To my beautiful son, the most magical day of my life was the day I became your mama. To my husband Mark, you are without a doubt, my other half. Thank you for your love and support. Lastly, thank you to my own mama who has never stopped loving and encouraging me in life.

19

THE BUSINESS OF MOM-BOSSING

by Shannon-Lee Figsby

"Some women suffer from postpartum depression. Not me. I had postpartum awakening."

Shannon-Lee Figsby

Shannon knew from a very young age that she wanted to spend her life creating. Her formal education came in the form of a bachelor's degree with a double-major in journalism and communications from Concordia University, while also spending nearly twenty years training for a career in professional dance.

Shannon is now the proud owner and director of the internationally recognized dance studio Academie de danse Elite Inc. in Ile Perrot, QC., home to the 2017 World Dance Champions. Shannon worked as a professional dancer for many years, appearing in many Montreal stage shows, commercials, and music videos. She is also a former professional CFL Cheerleader for the Montreal Alouettes.

After having her first child at the age of twenty-nine, and enduring an intense struggle to lose the seventy pounds she gained while pregnant with him, Shannon was compelled to start a second company called Fit Mama Shannon, which centered around health and wellness with a specific focus on helping women, particularly mothers, become their best selves. While she still adores working with and teaching youngsters, after becoming a mother herself, she knew she had a gift she could offer women who may be struggling like she was as well.

Shannon now owns a third company called Studio Couture, a dance and fitness wear company. Shannon is an Amazon top 100 best selling author of, *I'm 30, Now What?!* She lives in a suburb of Montreal, QC, with her husband, Chris and her two-year-old son, Dublin.

www.academiededanseelite.com | www.studio-couture.com
fb: academiededanseelite | fitmamashannon
wearestudiocouture | shannon.figsby
ig: @academiededanseelite | @fitmamashannon
@shannydancer | @wearestudiocouture

"I am not lucky. You know what I am? I am smart. I am talented. I take advantage of the opportunities that come my way and I work really, really hard. Don't call me lucky. Call me a badass."
~ Shonda Rhimes

I AM POSITIONED IN FRONT of a class of twenty one teenage girls aged thirteen to seventeen. I am trying desperately to lead a warm-up that includes ten minutes of dance cardio, followed by ten minutes of conditioning, stretching and abdominal work, before we get into another forty minutes of dance instruction. I have done this same warm-up, changing nothing but the songs, for the past seven years. But today, I am certain, I will die. I will not get through this warm-up alive.

Today, you see, I neglected to realize that actually, I have changed something other than the music. Today, as opposed to last time I gave a full-out dance class nearly one year ago, everything has changed.

Today, I am wearing three sports bras, and despite the triple bagging of my 36DDD's, my girls are aching with every kick-ball-change. Today, I am so exhausted that the simple act of breathing in air hurts my windpipe. Today, I am fifty pounds heavier than I was a year ago and I almost can't stand looking at myself in the mirror. Today, I have a new student – my four-week-old baby boy, who's watching me instruct the class from his bucket seat in the corner of the studio.

Today, I am not just a dance studio owner teaching a dance class. Today, I am also a mom. The problem is, everyone – including myself – seems to have forgotten that that last little differentiating factor is actually the biggest game changer that's ever existed.

That day, two and a half years ago, was a defining moment for me. Since we've been talking about the past, let me give you a little background.

For my entire life, the only thing I've ever wanted to do is dance. Perform, teach, own my own studio – I wanted it all. I started dancing at the age of three and never really stopped, competing until the end of high school and teaching and performing throughout university and the year that followed. When an opportunity arose to open my own dance school with a (now former) business partner eight years ago, I jumped all over it. All my dreams were coming true.

I poured my heart and soul, my blood, sweat, and tears, all my free time and energy, and sometimes, my own money, into Academie de danse Elite. It was my baby, and I was willing to do anything to see it flourish, and my students along with it. After I got engaged in 2013, people would ask me when I wanted to have kids. I would say I already have 250 of them. My students were like my surrogate children, and we were a family in our own right.

Until I gave birth to my own child in November of 2015, and realized that shit was about to get real.

I was determined not to let my status as a new mother affect my ability to run a growing company. I wanted to prove to everyone that I could do it all – be a wife, mother, and a badass business woman, and oh, guess what – I wasn't even going to put my kid in daycare. I could do it all. I would be a supermom. Who needs sleep?

What I didn't realize, however, was that by not accepting the significant and inevitable changes which come about as a result of bringing a baby into the mix, I was doing myself a huge disservice. I mean, no one should be teaching a dance class when they're still bleeding from their hoo-ha.

My son's first year on this earth was also the most challenging year for my studio, and brought about many changes that no one could have seen coming. And for this, I thank him. As I mentioned in my previous book that I co-authored, some women suffer from postpartum depression after giving birth. Not me. I had postpartum awakening.

There were so many moments where I wished I had someone to turn to – besides my amazing family, friends, and clients who became friends – for advice on how to balance this whole baby and business deal. So that's why I decided to write this chapter. Here, I'd like to share with you the top five things related to mom-ing and mom-bossing that I wished someone would have shared with me before having my son:

Your vision for the future of your business will become extremely clear. Go with it. For some, this may mean realizing the business world isn't for them. For me – this meant the total opposite. I dove in head first making changes in every single area of my studio that I thought would benefit my students – including buying out my business partner.

It's funny to think about it now, but before I had my son, I looked at other people's kids just like that – other people's kids. Becoming a mother added what I felt like was a new layer of responsibility to my job. I suddenly became vehemently passionate about not only the dance training my students were receiving, but also the *life lessons* I suddenly felt so graciously responsible to impart upon them. The fact that their parents were trusting me with this was no small thing.

I shifted the focus of the competitive program within my studio to mental preparation and coached my dancers more psychologically, than physically. There were small additions – like Pride Night before big competitions, where the girls dedicated their performance on stage the following day to someone who mattered deeply to them in their lives, to smaller ones such as distributing "Power Pak's" before competing with silly, but fun items like Ring Pops, bouncy balls, and other pun-allowing knick knacks.

I added a leadership program to the studio and shifted the focus of the teaching assistant program to one that wasn't just about getting free help, but also about giving our teaching assistants the tools necessary to become amazing teachers.

Looking at it now, I guess I started coaching my dancers exactly as I would want my son coached. Letting them know that no matter what, they were loved. Coming off stage after a less than stellar performance was no longer "good try," but "good job."

My approach worked. My first year owning the studio alone, we became the 2017 World Dance Champions, by far the biggest accomplishment of my career to date. And you know what? The person I was before having my son would not have that banner hanging in her studio. But that's okay. Because she didn't have the same priorities that I do. Because we were not the same person anymore.

Your priorities will change – and that's okay. Before I had my son, I had absolutely no qualms about working sixteen hour days and getting home from the studio at midnight. If there was work to be done, who cared if we ate dinner at midnight? My two equally top priorities were my clients, and ensuring my business was running as smoothly and efficiently as possible. Now, while the business is just as important, so is the business of bath time and bedtime stories.

The fact is, as much as you might want to tell yourself that you're the same person you were before having a baby, you aren't. You, quite simply, are not. And that's not a bad thing. You've brought a new life into this world, and that new life is bringing some new perspective to yours.

Personally, this hit me hard. It particularly hit me hard in the body image department. As a dancer, your livelihood is directly impacted by your appearance. It's just a reality of the industry. If you have a tendency towards the extreme, as I do, this reality can lead to an unhealthy obsession with being thin, and in my case, an eating disorder that lasted nearly a decade.

However, as I mentioned in my previous book, *I'm 30, Now What?!* - when you become pregnant as a recovering anorexic, you do not restrict yourself. No matter what you think you need, becoming a mama is about what the baby needs. And for me, that started in the womb.

So I ate for nine months. I mean, gawd did I eat! Everything and anything I wanted or had denied myself for the better portion of my adolescent and adult life. Seventy pounds later, I gave birth to a beautiful, healthy, and very average sized 7.2 lb baby boy. The rest was all me!

But after having Dublin, for the first time in my life, I wasn't in a massive rush to lose the weight. Unlike many women (whom I'm not judging – you do you!) who start exercising at the six-week postpartum mark once their doctor has given them the green light, I preferred the six-month mark, hence the near-death experience teaching a bunch of teenagers I described earlier.

Whereas the pre-baby me was hiking three days after major knee surgery to avoid "sluggishness" aka weight gain, the post-baby Shannon simply had other priorities. One major priority was being able to produce enough breast milk to continue nursing my son as long as I wanted to, so calorie restriction wasn't an option. And for those first few months, I'd choose sleep over working out. In. A. Freaking. Heartbeat.

Dublin was born in November, 2015 and I lost the first ten pounds in May, 2016. While the baby weight is now gone completely, the healthy habits are here to stay. Not just for myself, but as an example for my son and future children of a mom who prioritizes health over all else, regardless of the circumstances.

You actually, really, cannot do it all. Get some help. Figure out two things about your business right away – what you LOVE doing, and what can ONLY be done by you. Delegate the rest. Hire office staff. Hire a cleaning person. Heck, do the same for your house if you can afford it (I couldn't at first). Do the same with a meal service. Do what you have to do so you can spend your time on things you love to do such as running your business and being with your family.

If you're anything like me, the word "delegate" makes you shudder. Embrace the shivers, Mama. I know. I KNOW you think that you are the only person who can draft a reminder email perfectly, choose and order the most exquisite costume, and ensure it's expertly sized on 456 children, AND keep desk accessories in your office exactly how they should be, and you might be right. But you know what's better than perfect?

Done.

Not just done, but done and home, with my son and husband, enjoying their company instead of stressing over what looms unfinished at the studio.

Although delegating was difficult for me, it was made easier after identifying what it was about my business that I was truly passionate about – what filled my cup. For me, it was always the interaction I had with the students and their parents. So communication became my focus, and my main one at that. Everything, and I mean everything, that wasn't completely student-centric or had a direct impact on the interpersonal relationships with the people I surrounded myself with every day became the responsibility of someone else. Teachers were asked to choose their own costumes and complete size measurements for their students, and then submit their data to me. I hired an accounting firm that did everything via that famous cloud somewhere out there in cyberspace. I mean, all I had to do was snap a picture of a receipt or invoice with my phone and POOF – look Ma, accounting's done! I hired a law firm I only needed to meet with once a year to keep the minute book of my corporation up to date, legally.

For every responsibility, I had a "guy" (or girl!) who could do it for me, so I could focus on what I really loved doing. Besides, nobody's good at everything anyways, and if they claim to be, they're too good to be true.

Be real – other moms will love you more for it. In the early days of having my son, I was so afraid my clients would perceive becoming a mother as a weakness since I was the "get it done" partner in the studio. This was probably the same mentality that led me to believe I had to resume teaching classes four weeks postpartum. How wrong I was. Who are my clients? Kids. What do kids have? Moms. Moms who have been there, moms who see the struggle, and moms who see through the bullshit if you claim there are no struggles. These are your people.

I found my people in the place I knew best – my own studio. The sisterhood of mothers is one that I quickly found transcends age, language, socio-economic status, and even client-service provider relationships.

I vividly remember the day I walked out of the studio and into the hallway smack dab in the middle of a class I was teaching. My period was back for the first time since having my child, and it was back with a vengeance. Seeing the horror on my face, one mom in her mid-fifties asked what was wrong.

"The super-sized tampon I was wearing just fell straight out of my vagina," I told her, completely serious. "Is this normal during your first postpartum period?"

She assured me it was, and that I could expect many other fun surprises I hadn't yet been warned about, like having this period last weeks on end (it did), and peeing every time I laughed (I don't – but give me time, I only have one kid!).

The thing is, she didn't even bat an eye. This was the same mom who I had always been somewhat intimidated by – a police officer with a straightforward attitude and strong opinions she frequently made known. Because she had been there, and like me, she was not afraid to be real about it. Because she was my people.

My son found a surrogate family within the walls of my studio, quite literally. And in turn, I found my mom tribe. I nearly lost my shit one afternoon when my son was about eleven months old and starting his first bout of gastroenteritis. I was feeding him, when all of a sudden he stood up on my thighs, looked me in the eyes, and projectile vomited straight into my face. And then did it again. I was covered in vomit, quite literally from head to waist, concerned for my son while at the same time on the verge of tears, considering I felt as if my dignity as a studio owner was hanging by a thread. I should mention this was about three weeks after my former business partner and I split, and I purchased the studio! But before I could lose it completely, a studio-mom swooped in, took my son and stripped him while passing him off to another mom. As she sent her daughter to get me some clothes from the merchandise table, she wiped the vomit from my face and hair while instructing her son to start scrubbing the carpets. She sent me home swiftly, and when I came in the next day, there was no evidence of anything that had happened the night before. While this particular mom and her entire family have become dear, dear friends of mine, it was so crystal clear to me in that moment, I was surrounded by love.

Be real Mama, and the authenticity will come back to you in spades.

You will figure out what works for you. If you are anything like me, you were winging your child's first year of life. Maybe you still are. The fact that my studio is open at night posed a particular set of issues for our little family considering the fact that I was still nursing, a "normal" sleep schedule wasn't possible, and so many other factors. However, eventually, we got into a groove and figured out what worked for us. My son came to work with me every single day and still does, until Dad, Grammy, or Nanny picks him up for dinner and bedtime a few nights a week. He is surrounded by other kids and I'll never have to look for a babysitter as long as I live. And he gets to see first hand that it's not just the dads' who get to be CEOs... His mama isn't doing so bad herself!

And neither are you. After all, you've got this, Mama!

~ For both my mom and my son,
for teaching me how to be a mother.

20

CHANGING OURSELVES AND THE WORLD THROUGH PARENTING

by Sunit Suchdev

"I say no to what doesn't serve me."

Sunit Suchdev

Sunit Suchdev has always been a natural born leader and knew that inspiring others was her mission. Starting as a gymnastics coach at the age of thirteen, she has spent many years of her life coaching those around her in some capacity. A self-proclaimed research and health junkie, she spends much of her free time with her nose in health books or self-help books. She is a podcast host and speaker who inspires moms to prepare better for motherhood, parent with purpose, and raise amazing kids without losing themselves.

After experiencing endless personal struggle and loss, including infertility, miscarriages, and the deaths of loved ones within a short time, she has grown into a woman who believes that light makes darkness disappear, and anything is possible when you have gratitude, and a plan. With the right mindset, mothers can truly thrive, instead of just survive.

Sunit wants to change the world through moms. She holds a university degree and various certifications in the areas of business, leadership, mindset, health and wellness, and is a certified life coach and meditation teacher. She loves essential oils, blue drinks, and of course, her hubby and twin boys, who drive her to live a life of excellence.

www.sunitsuchdev.com
ig: @sunitsuchdev
fb: SunitSuchdev

"The choice to become a mother is the choice to become
one of the greatest spiritual teachers there is."
~ Oprah Winfrey

WHEN I WAS a little girl, my dad would always check the weather forecast before we went to school. He wanted to ensure we were dressed appropriately for the day, and anticipate any changes ahead of time so that we were prepared. This was my dad in a nutshell. He instilled in us from a very young age that one should always be prepared for what life brings. According to my dad, there were rarely good excuses for not anticipating what was to come. We learned to ask questions and listen to those who had walked the same path so we could be informed. We learned to research and read up on things we didn't know anything about, and of course, we learned to check the weather every single day. This seemingly benign trait of my dad's would serve me well as I entered motherhood, and to this day, is one of the guiding principles in my life. Always be prepared, willing to learn, and do better. This is empowerment.

It should go without saying then, that this epidemic we have, of moms who are being completely bowled over by motherhood, and losing themselves, is confusing to me. Why are we surprised by how difficult motherhood is? Entering into this most important job, we should be more prepared than any other job in life. And yet, many moms, are not. Unfortunately, this trickles into our children, and it affects them on a deep level. The divide and social unrest we are seeing in the world today, are a result of deep rooted issues which start with how we are being raised.

When I became pregnant with twins, I started paying careful attention to what moms were saying to me about motherhood, and I made a choice. Instead of saying, "That won't be me," or "I don't want that to be me," I learned to ask, "HOW can I ensure this isn't me?" I heard stories of women losing themselves in the process, and putting their husbands on the backburner. Women who brought babies home and weren't able to handle how life had changed. Women who were struggling with postpartum depression or were so riddled with stress and anxiety that it was having a physical impact on their health. So, I essentially launched into doing what my dad instilled in me from a young age. I thought ahead about what could potentially go wrong, and I put an action plan in place on how to try and avoid it. I wanted to THRIVE, not just survive, in motherhood. If you pay attention at all to anyone who is already a mom, you will know that becoming a parent is a HUGE decision. Not only are you about to embark on one of the most difficult jobs of your life, one for which there is no manual, and one where you must start off completely sleep deprived, but it is also up to you to ensure that this human being becomes a productive member of society.

The hard part about parenting is actually not the sleep deprivation or getting them to eat their vegetables. The hard part about parenting is thinking ahead about the gravity of raising a great human, and knowing the little steps you will take every day, seven days a week, three hundred and sixty five days a year, to ensure this happens. It is parenting with intention and purpose, and giving careful consideration to everything you say, every choice you make, every action you take, that is difficult.

It takes preparation and awareness to thrive, and not just survive, as a mother.

Many years ago, before my kids were born, my mom was diagnosed with a cancer which was scary as hell, but she eventually ended up beating it. Shortly after, my mother-in-law was diagnosed with MS. These were little whispers in my life. They nudged me. They were a nice reminder as I prepared for motherhood that I need to be healthy and whole to be there for others and that I needed to nurture myself so I was always able to be in a place of service for my children.

My dad passed away recently, and his death was the ultimate irony because after living a life of preparedness, it is not something he was prepared for. After living a healthy sixty-eight years, he was suddenly diagnosed with a terminal brain cancer. Although I am a grown woman with children of my own, I still need my dad. Those whispers from years ago, have now become a shout. So now, more than ever, I am passionate not only about not losing myself, but ensuring that my cup is filled in every way so I can be fully present for my children for as long as possible. How you care for your mind, body, and soul, will impact if and how you can show up for your family. These parts of you need to be nurtured because, you simply cannot give what you yourself do not possess. When women say they feel guilty about taking time for self-care, I wonder what they think self-care really means. It doesn't mean you care for yourself at the expense of your children. It means you love your children enough to care for that which is most important to them. YOU.

Taking time early on in your parenthood journey to establish what YOU need to nurture yourself, and ensuring you have a plan to be able to do that on a regular basis, will serve you well. Think of it like an anchor. You cannot get lost when you are anchored down, strong in who you are, and know exactly what you need to remain that person. You cannot forget to care for yourself when you already have an established routine.

After my dad's death, I also started studying mindfulness and meditation. My dad, although a very healthy man, was the kind of guy whose brain never turned off. I have a sneaking suspicion that stress may have played a part in the tumor he developed. There is much research now to show that stress is as bad as sugar for you. I learned that when we stop trying to juggle all the balls, and just mindfully focus on one thing at a time, we physiologically affect how our brain is working. We lower our blood pressure and decrease stress hormones. After all the little nudges towards the life I'm living today, my dad's death was the ultimate catalyst for me to delve EVEN deeper into my true purpose in life. I no longer want to be surrounded by sickness and overwhelm, which seem to be rampant amongst moms today. There are so many ways we can intercept this path by inspiring and empowering moms to live a life full of vitality, health, and purpose while teaching their kids to do the same. I have slowly morphed into a spiritual, health conscious, crunchy momma who meditates and takes time for self care every single day. I've learned to say "no" to what doesn't serve me and am the least busy person I know. I feel no guilt and am happy all the time. This is not by accident. Guilt arises when you are out of alignment. I don't feel guilty for prioritizing myself because I know that it allows me to show up fully and benefits my kids more than if I were to try to parent them from a place of lack. Guilt comes from feeling like you are making the wrong choice. When you put in the work to really get anchored in yourself and then start to parent with intention, you will know you are on the right path because you will feel little guilt.

As I move through motherhood, I realize my passion is to help moms get to a place where they talk about all the amazing things they are doing, instead of what they are not getting done. This happens by shifting our mindset, incorporating self care, and coming up with a parenting plan, among other things. If, right now, you are thinking, *Yes I'll take some of that please!*, I have a podcast you can listen to each week to feel inspired in all areas of life and motherhood. I also offer a course you can take to get into the right mindset, and provide one-on-one life coaching for moms wanting a guide in doing that deep work. Motherhood doesn't have to be hard. I'm the happiest mom I know. I have an attitude of gratitude and find it difficult to maintain relationships with those who don't. Yet, I remain steadfast in my belief that most moms want to get there, so I'm hoping to inspire them. Imagine if every mom took such great care of herself that she was raising like-minded kids who would grow up to create massive change in the world? What you focus on, expands. So when you make your SELF a priority, you will grow, and your growth will in turn help you grow great kids. I believe this is my calling. Our world needs health, love, and light. Children who are growing up open minded, and grounded. This is the change we need to see.

In Dr Shefali Tsabary's book, *The Conscious Parent,* she reminds us that our children do not belong to us. They are spiritual beings who need guidance to become what they are put on this earth to become. As much as they need us to guide them, we also need them to guide US. Essentially, our children are our teachers. The relationship between mother and child is so sacred, but not for the reasons we think. What a special privilege it is to be chosen as the person who will help this little human become a productive member of society, but more importantly, someone who is healthy and whole enough to unlock their own purpose and share their gifts with the world. Allowing a mutual exchange of learning between ourselves and our children can be a beautiful life

experience. I look at all the adults walking around today, deeply trou-
bled and in pain. Adults who have not been raised with intention and
purpose, and now need to spend years in therapy undoing the damage
that was done. They are now raising children of their own. Until we stop
this cycle, the world will continue on the path it is on.

I especially related to Dr. Tsabary because I'm an Indian woman
who comes from a culture where traditions, and what people will think,
outweigh what is truly best for us, as does she. She talks about coming
to the United States at a young age to escape the pressures of growing
up in such a restrictive culture. Whether you are of Indian heritage or
not, I think everyone can relate to growing up with a certain compass.
Your parents set this compass. You grow up believing what you were
taught to believe based on what THEY were taught to believe. So if
THEY are wounded and have not done the deep work themselves, then
of course, they are influencing that in you. So I look to myself today
and know that I can stop this cycle. I do not want my children to leave
home at twenty years of age and spend the next ten years "finding"
themselves. They wouldn't have to find themselves if we did a good job
from day one and helped them actually grow into who they are meant
to become. We cannot, however, do that if we ourselves are lost.

It's never too late to unlearn the things that have held you back,
and create new rules for yourself. Nor is it too late to become the person you want to be. When we allow ourselves to heal, and rewrite our
own stories, we are able to fully step into motherhood in an authentic
way. That, my friends, is self care.

I have done the deep work and realized that I am in control. In
control of my happiness, my life, my thoughts, and most importantly,
I am empowered to do whatever it takes to raise children who will become who they are meant to be. And they will get there faster than I
did. When you do this kind of work, you feel confident. This is what is
missing today. We are all looking outside of ourselves for the answers to
life, including how to be a good parent. In reality, we need to be looking
inwards. What are the things you value and how will you instill these in
your children? How will you ensure your children are growing up happy,
healthy, and well balanced? What are the qualities and morals you want
them to possess? These are the things we should be thinking about
from early on. Start at the end and move backwards.

Let's say you want to raise a child who is a professional hockey player. In order to give them even a shot at this opportunity, you need to be introducing them to that sport very early on. It's the same with everything. For me personally, I wanted to raise children who are mindful. Children who are respectful, and kind. I wanted to raise kids who have a great love for food, especially healthy food. I want kids who will spread light and love everywhere they go. I want to raise kids who do not reach for medications, drugs, or alcohol at the first sign of physical or emotional pain, but rather have the tools they need to deal with the root cause. Knowing this ahead of time has helped me to start off my parenting journey on the right foot. I talk to the people whose children exemplify these qualities and I read the books that help me cultivate them. I parent intentionally.

I recently read a powerful Facebook post by a local health coach who pointed out how many of us are struggling to lose weight and keep our bodies healthy as adults. This is the case because we were not started off on the right foot by our own parents, and deeply ingrained habits are hard to break. Knowing this, why would we not do everything it takes to avoid our children growing up and having to go through the same difficulties? If we can save them from the difficult task of undoing bad habits, why wouldn't we? Of course, this is in reference to food, but I think it is a metaphor for everything. Give your children the gift of a happy, healthy mom, first and foremost, and then start them off on the right foot in every way.

I have taught my children to meditate because I know this will help them self regulate, be more mindful, and be more grounded. I eat healthy food and raise them in a home where there is no other way so they will grow up feeling good and appreciate real food. When they are not feeling well, I reach for essential oils and talk about what may be causing their pain so they grow up with natural remedies and an understanding of how their bodies function. I put myself first so they will grow up with a healthy and happy mom who is fulfilled and full of light, and they will go on to reap the benefits and do the same. I prioritize my marriage and allow them to see that so they will grow up not believing they are the center of our universe, but instead, realize that the key to a healthy, happy family is parents who love each other first. These things are what we do in our family because they are the steps to raising the kinds of kids WE want to raise. They may or may not be priorities for you. I encourage you to figure out what YOUR priorities are and then do the work it takes to parent with intention so you can thrive as a mother, and raise the amazing kids you were meant to raise.

When you do all this work, something else wonderful happens. You stop looking at what everyone else is doing. You feel confident that you are doing what is best for YOU and YOUR family, and you don't compare yourself with other moms. Often times, we look at others and wonder how they have it all together. Or we judge and assume that they don't. When you realize that the most important thing we can do is be fulfilled in our own lives by knowing what is truly important to US, we can stop comparing ourselves to, and judging others. The perfect mom that you see on Pinterest IS perfect. She's perfect for HER family. Perfection is subjective. If you are hitting the goals you set for yourself and your kids, then you are hitting perfection. Figure out what's important to YOU and parent according to THAT.

To summarize, there is a method to this madness. It can actually be broken down into three basic steps:

Be prepared. Parenthood is not for the faint of heart, and as Dr, Tsabary says, our world could actually do with a bit of a break right now. Everyone is having children without giving real thought to what this means. It is the most important job in the world, and you should prepare for it as such.

Get anchored in who you are and prioritize yourself FIRST. Know what it takes to stay healthy, in your mind, body, and soul. Then take steps to do that every day so you can thrive, and not just survive, as a mom.

Have a solid understanding of what kinds of kids you want to raise, and the obstacles you faced in your own life so you can avoid your children having to go through them, and then reverse engineer to come up with a parenting plan that works for you. Then, implement it. Every. Single. Day. Be intentional in your parenting and feel confident that you have truly done the work and know what you are doing as a parent.

When you follow these steps, you will feel more grounded in your parenting choices and less likely to cave to the pressure and comments from others. When strangers, your friends, your in-laws, or your child's friend's parents say things that make you question what you're doing, you will need to remind yourself that you are parenting your kids according to the way YOU want to raise them. You will also need to remember that when others point out your shortcomings, it's not about you. It's actually about them. Nothing anyone ever says or does is because of you. You are simply their mirror, reflecting back to them where they may be falling short themselves. This concept is SO important to remember in life, especially in motherhood. Give yourself grace and kindness. You will make mistakes, but they are yours to reconcile, and no one else's. Don't take advice from, or give in to the criticisms of, people who have not been where you want to go. I always look to the moms who look like they are rocking it and raising amazing kids. *They* are who I surround myself with. *They* are who I take tips from.

What the world needs now is change. True change comes from taking inspired action. My social responsibility begins within the four walls of my home. How can I make change anywhere else if I can't make it within myself and my family? When I work on changing myself, I'm also affecting my children, and that is how we can all contribute. I'm hoping to change the world through moms. I'm starting with mySELF. I hope you will join me.

~ I would like to dedicate this chapter to the love of my life, my husband. I would be nowhere without your love and never ending support.

FINAL THOUGHTS

FEATURING
Sabrina Greer and Linda Greer

If children live with criticism, they learn to condemn.
If children live with hostility, they learn to fight.
If children live with fear, they learn to be apprehensive.
If children live with pity, they learn to feel sorry for themselves.
If children live with ridicule, they learn to feel shy.
If children live with jealousy, they learn to feel envy.
If children live with shame, they learn to feel guilty.
If children live with encouragement, they learn confidence.
If children live with tolerance, they learn patience.
If children live with praise, they learn appreciation.
If children live with acceptance, they learn to love.
If children live with approval, they learn to like themselves.
If children live with recognition, they learn it is good to have a goal.
If children live with sharing, they learn generosity.
If children live with honesty, they learn truthfulness.
If children live with fairness, they learn justice.
If children live with kindness and consideration, they learn respect.
If children live with security,
they learn to have faith in themselves and in those about them.
If children live with friendliness,
they learn the world is a nice place in which to live.

~ *Children Learn What They Live* by Dorothy Law Nolte, Ph.D.

IN THE OPENING OF THIS BOOK, I mentioned that initially it was to be a collection of data and summarized interviews, retold stories about the meaning of motherhood. I also mentioned that it evolved and became something so much more powerful and compelling. I did, however, still interview one mama whose story I will share as the closing words on what I can only imagine has been as much an emotional journey for you reading this collection, as it was for us, writing.

This mama has more experience than the likes of us combined. She has undergone the hardships of loss, dealt with the let downs of things not going according to plan, the temporary insanity of the fourth trimester with one very strong-willed, colicky baby girl. This woman cared for dozens of non-biological children in her home, and over the span of two decades, raised the equivalent of multiple middle school classrooms, full time. She dealt with all the mentioned emotions, showed remarkable strength and courage, and is now a beloved grandmother to three gorgeous little boys. I cannot think of a better message to tie these stories together. I may be biased however, as I am referring to my own mother.

I wanted to better understand the circle of life. What is the outcome of these grandiose lessons we are learning? What is it like to see your baby, have babies? If you could send messages of empowerment and wisdom back to your pregnant self, your new-mom self, and at every stage thereafter and in-between, what would those be? I had so many questions that the content started to develop into a chapter all of its own, into a book of its own, even. I wanted to stay true to the story much like the rest of the chapters in this book. So rather than ghostwriting her memoirs, I left her story as is, in all its raw and beautiful glory. I learned many things about my mother throughout this journey (including the fact that she can write), but surprisingly, I also learned a lot about myself. My mother just turned sixty-years-old and this is her first published piece. Please enjoy.

❤ ❤ ❤

Time! What a complicated thing! *They* say, "Time flies" or "Don't blink, because you'll miss something." I never completely understood the truth to this until I had children of my own. It seems like just yesterday, I was standing in front of the Minister saying, "I do" and here I am, forty-two years and thirty-four kids later, and I just celebrated my sixtieth birthday. In my head, it's still 1975, and I should be going to another Led Zeppelin or Pink Floyd concert, but instead, I just spent the weekend taking care of my grandkids (mind you, equally as entertaining and exciting), but how did I get here? I guess the simple answer is: One day at a time. You get out of bed, put your best foot forward, and appreciate every day, knowing that even if today doesn't go according to plan, tomorrow is always a fresh start.

I should probably explain the numbers I just mentioned. Anyone capable of doing simple math must be wondering if this is a typo, or if old age is getting to me. If I just turned sixty, yes, that means I was eighteen years old when I got married. You also read correctly that I have been a mother to thirty-four children. One biological child (who just happens to be the lead author of this book), three adopted children and thirty (yes thirty) foster children, some who were part of our family for only a few days, and others who were with us for many years.

Getting married right after high school, I thought I knew exactly what I wanted to do with my life and having kids was not it (thank God, because I was still a kid myself). I wanted to be a fur-mama and save animals, all of them. I got a job cleaning kennels and mopping floors at the Toronto Humane Society. I joined the Save The Whales and Save The Seals foundations and was ready to take on the world. It wasn't until years later, when I was promoted to a position of authority that I realized, anytime you're dealing with living things, there will be sickness and death parallel to the joys and triumphs. After seeing more than my fair share of tragedy, I decided to take a break, an indefinite break. My husband had a great job with excellent benefits, so I took some much needed time to regroup.

I was only twenty-three years old, and we had just bought our first home. Suddenly, I had an overwhelming desire to become a mother. I was an only child, and I knew it took my parents nine years of trying to conceive before getting pregnant with me. I figured it would be best to start trying right away. To my surprise, we got pregnant after only four months. Going for that ultrasound and hearing the heartbeat for the first time, you would think I would be overjoyed, but instead, I felt terrified. My first reaction was, *What the hell have we done? I know nothing about babies.*

As I mentioned earlier, I was an only child. I had never even held a baby before, let alone cared for one. It took weeks for it to sink in that this was happening. I was finally coming to terms with the whole thing, when I woke up in a pool of blood one morning. We rushed to the hospital and had an emergency ultrasound, the heartbeat that was there before could no longer be heard. A few weeks earlier, I wasn't even sure I wanted this baby, and now, there was nothing I wanted more.

In the days and weeks to come, I felt bombarded with people's condolences and words of wisdom. "It's not uncommon to lose your first baby," "You can always try again," "So sorry for your loss, but I know how you feel." I felt guilty as though it were my fault for not wanting this baby right away, but ultimately, you must trust the powers that be. We decided to wait six months after having the D&C (Dilation and curettage is a brief surgical procedure in which the cervix is dilated and a special instrument is used to scrape the uterine lining), *I know, lovely,* before we started trying again, and to our surprise, got pregnant almost immediately.

This time I was overjoyed, *This is how it is supposed to feel*, it dawned on me that perhaps I lost my first baby so I could experience this sense of wonder and appreciation, free of doubts and regrets. Although I was elated to be pregnant, at the back of my mind was that ever-present fear and anxiety of having another miscarriage.

After getting through the first trimester with no complications, I was enjoying the second trimester. Experiencing all the firsts I hadn't with my previous pregnancy. The baby moving, feeling hiccups and kicks from within was a cause for celebration. Then the third trimester hit! I was feeling exhausted and started gaining weight, a lot of weight. Everyone including the doctors said it was perfectly normal and not to worry. My ankles started to look more like my thighs, *Not that I could see either.* We went back to the doctor and sure enough, "toxemic pregnancy," "bed rest," and "high-risk" all became new words in my vocabulary, and my new reality. Remember, this was long before the days of Google searches and mommy chat rooms. I spent my months on (not so restful) bed-rest reading medical journals and books on toxemia.

I had gained over eighty pounds (*yes, I said eighty, this is yet again crazy, but correct math),* before they dropped the bomb that I would be induced the next day due to preeclampsia. The induction process was grueling. Twenty-four hours of on again, off again, labor before my "specialist" came in and said, "We have to get this baby delivered, I have other appointments to get to." So, he turned up the Pitocin, gave me an epidural, and off we went. I don't remember too much after that point. The details of my birth experience would come from the testimonies of delivery nurses almost a year later, at the malpractice hearing. All I knew was when I woke up after having three units of transfused blood, I was missing half my uterus, and had over twenty stitches piecing me together. That's when my husband told me we had a beautiful, healthy, baby girl and for a moment, all was good.

While I was elated, I was equally as devastated. Just as I was an only child, my baby girl would be too. How could this happen? This was a doctor who did this to me, someone we entrust with our bodies and our well-being. Someone who had taken an oath "to do no harm." Months later, I found out that I was not his only victim; some of the poor women who had trusted him had actually lost their lives at his hand. I felt grateful just to be alive. What would my husband have done if I hadn't made it off that delivery table? What would have happened to my sweet baby girl growing up without a mother? All that mattered was that incredible life I held in my arms.

I spent ten days in the hospital trying to heal the best I could. Nurses were waking me every few hours to attach this screaming little person to my breast; I spent the rest of the time on the toilet peeing out sixty pounds of water weight after they pumped me full of diuret-ics. *Sorry if this is TMI, as the kids say.*

Finally, they said I could go home. Again, I was hit with a flood of mixed emotions. I couldn't believe they were going to let me walk out the door with this innocent baby, sure they had shown me how to bathe her and change her. Breastfeeding was going reasonably well. *Were they crazy? How was I supposed to keep this tiny human alive without their help?*

The next few months turned out to be just as scary and overwhelm-ing as I had anticipated. This beautiful innocent baby girl did nothing but cry, and cry, and CRY. The only time she stopped crying was when she was attached to my breast. I showered, slept, went to the bath-room, and ate with her attached to me, most of the time, with both of us crying. Yes, I was one of the lucky ones to have a colicky baby. I just kept thinking, *Haven't I suffered through enough?* All I wanted was to have a happy baby. It wasn't until years later I realized just how incred-ibly lucky and blessed I was, because you see, all those challenges and phases are just temporary, and just as time passes so rapidly, so do the phases. Trust me!

So, I blinked just like "they" told me not to. My daughter was about to start school, and I was going to be all alone all day. I had spent the last four years devoting my time and attention to her, and now she was walking out the door to get on a school bus and leaving me by myself. Despite all the heartache, in the beginning, I wanted to do this all over again. I wanted to have another baby; I wanted my daughter to grow up with siblings, but how? That is when a friend of my husband's told us about foster parenting. He was a foster child himself and had been adopted by his foster parents at a very young age. This was a way of bypassing the long waiting lists for adoption; we could have a baby in just a few months. All we had to do is fill out some paperwork and take some training courses. A piece of cake!

Of course, no one told us most of these kids (even the newborn ba-bies), come with tons of baggage; physical, emotional, and sometimes even harmful addictions. That, oddly enough, was not the hardest part of fostering. Dealing with the Children's Aid and the biological parents proved to be quite challenging, but letting go of a child who had become part of your family for a month, a year, or sometimes even longer, was devastating.

These kids need so much more from you than an average child; more time and attention; more love and kindness. And even after pouring your heart and soul, day and night into caring for these kids, sometimes, you would only get days' notice about them leaving. So why did we keep doing it for almost thirty years, you ask? I think it was the lives we touched, the lives we forever changed. We were able to adopt three beautiful babies, two boys, one with Attention Deficit Hyperactivity Disorder (ADHD) and chronic asthma, the other with Asperger Syndrome (autism), and a beautiful baby girl with Fetal Alcohol Syndrome. As for the other thirty or so children, we had little say in what became of their journey. Some went to wonderful adoptive families, others ended up back in the unfortunate situation they arrived from. You learn to accept the things you cannot change and be grateful for the situations you can. If I made even one child's life better, than it was all worth it.

At the onset of being foster parents, I felt the same apprehension as I did when we brought Sabrina home from the hospital, every time a worker showed up at our door. As time went on, however, I started to look forward to that knock (even when it was the middle of the night). Every new life I was entrusted with was the start of a new adventure, equal in its challenges and rewards. Syndromes and disorders I had never heard of before, soon became part of my everyday life. Unfortunately, the majority of the problems these children encountered, were all too preventable. We saw a lot of fetal alcohol syndrome and horrific drug withdrawals. Some challenging mental health issues such as bipolar disorder and schizophrenia came through our doors. It is no surprise that the children who were the hardest to find homes for were those with invisible disabilities and mental health issues.

People often asked me, "How do you do it, deal with so many kids with such special needs?" My reply was always, "With lots of help." I was fortunate enough to have my husband who worked the night shift and was home all day to help. My father lived with us and was there at a moment's notice to lend a hand. My best friend (who was more like a sister to me) came over to help with the kids all the time. Then there was my "village," the endless parade of professionals coming in and out of our lives when we needed them most. Pediatricians, specialists, therapists, psychiatrists, resource teachers, and the E.A.s, were just some the many people to help, if I were ever to reach out.

You are not expected to do this on your own; it does take a village to raise a child.

Even with the help of my village, the day to day chaos was all mine to either embrace or let drive me crazy. We always had a plaque hanging on our wall with the poem by Dorothy Law Nolte, titled, *Children Learn What They Live,* and every time I was about to lose it, I would read her words of wisdom and remember all those little eyes were on me, looking to me for guidance and love. My most important job was to be the best version of myself, and set a good example for them. That's not to say I never made mistakes, because I made many, but I was always truthful, explained what I had done wrong, apologized, and always expected the same from them.

At some point during all the chaos, I must have blinked again, because those special kids were now special teenagers. There were ten years between my eldest (Sabrina) and our youngest, but that meant I had four teenagers at the same time. It is a proven fact that when the body reaches adolescence, hormones are released into the brain and cause a literal chemical imbalance, call it temporary insanity. I thought all my experience with mental illness would have prepared me for what was to come. As it turns out, the best strategy I had for dealing with teenagers was empathy. Remembering what it felt like for everything to be so confusing and dramatic. The simplest things seemed like the end of the world.

Teenagers are very much like toddlers, they need limits, boundaries, and positive consequences. The deal I had with all my kids was as long as they were honest, we could get through anything. The word got out and before long it wasn't just my kids coming to me for help, it was their friends as well. Our home became the "safe house," where the neighborhood teenagers would come when they felt they had nowhere else to go. We even had a few of our kids' friends move in with us for a while when they were having problems. As hard as it was at times not to freak out, I always tried to stay calm and listen, really listen! Any child of any age only ever wants to be heard, understood, and accepted for who they are: An individual. From a toddler trying to say their first word to an emotional teenager trying to express their extremely complicated feelings, the most important thing we can give them as parents is unconditional love, a safe place to be themselves and speak their minds.

All my kids are now adults. What I have learned from all my years of parenting is we may call them OUR children, but they do not belong to us. They are their own beings with their own free will, whether they are our biological children, adopted children, foster children, or stepchildren, they will all grow up someday and be out there in the world on their own. A friend of mine (another foster mom), had identical twin girls. These two grew up in the same home with the same parents, went to the same school, even had the same teachers and group of friends, but as adults, they lead very different lives (but that's another story). This is where free will comes in. We all make choices that will affect our lives and have circumstances that are sometimes out of our control. This is what shapes our lives, some call it fate. Little did I know all those years ago when I found out I couldn't have more children, that I would go on to be a foster parent and improve the lives of thirty-three non-biological children. All we can hope to do as parents is, the best we can, be good people, and set a good example, but in the end, unconditional love will always prevail.

In my experience, it's every parent's wish that their children have a better life than their own, but for me, I can only hope that my children find the joy and fulfillment that I have experienced being their mother. There is no greater feeling than helping others; making a difference in just one person's life can potentially change the world. I am so incredibly proud of my daughter, of the woman she has become, but even more than that, the mother she has become to my three amazing grandsons. They are my greatest gift in life. I feel as though my parenting journey has come full circle, now I can watch the power of unconditional love be passed on to the next generation. I hope that by finding her voice and sharing the incredible stories of the women in this book, we can touch the lives of even more mothers out there, who can in return take the wisdom, raise amazing kids, and shape the next generation. We are here to prove to you that, "You've Got This, Mama!"

❤ ❤ ❤

So there you have it. The evolution of motherhood. Fear can forever be present if you allow it. It is okay to be scared, but you must trust your instincts and truly believe, with every fiber, that you've got this. Motherhood is almost entirely comprised of unknowns, even when you have more than one child, as every experience is different, every child is different. You can allow the fear and unknown to take hold of you or you can embrace this beautiful chaos for what it is - temporary - and enjoy living every moment in the present.

Having children myself, whose ages span a decade, as my eldest is entering adolescence, I am constantly reminded of this; it is not just the uncomfortable and the madness that is temporary, it is every fleeting moment as well. It is their youth and the juvenile excitement and joy that so naturally surface in children over the smallest things. It is in those beautiful moments where you can feel your heart stretch and fill with love; be reminded of this light in the dark times. You see, everything through the eyes of an infant or a toddler is also unknown, they just have not been influenced by external pressures, that invite the presence of fear.

In the words of Marianne Williamson, one of my biggest inspirations, *"Love is what we were born with, fear is what we learned here."*

Fear is psychological, meaning it is created in our minds, compounded over time by a combination of external and internal pressures. As mothers, we fear failure, judgement, our capabilities, losing our identities and, of course, the unknown. It is okay to be afraid. Dance with these fears, face them head on and embrace them for a moment before gently releasing them. We really need not sweat the small stuff. As for the not so small stuff, we need to have faith and trust we are on our rightful path. We must believe this is the "plan" and take every challenge as an opportunity for growth.

It is no secret that motherhood is full of challenges. This book and its authors have certainly not candy-coated that position. If one lesson could be pulled from the hearts and souls poured all over these pages, let it be to parent with love and live with love; pure, simple, fierce, and unconditional love. Love these little people with all you've got and when you have achieved that, love them some more. Love can quell sadness, diminish anger, and fill your heart with joy. Love can heal pain, repair damage, and create positive change in the world. We can teach our children to live in love and not fear, and teach them we must because most of all, love conquers fear and sets the foundation for the future.

With hearts full of love, from all of us to you, You've Got This, Mama.

~ I would like to dedicate this book to all of the moms out there that are building a better world and future through these tiny humans. A huge shout out to my own mother for inspiring me to be the woman and mama I am today. Thank you to Brad, my love, for your (almost always) unwavering support and friendship and of course to my boys, Oliver, Sterling, and Walker, without you, I would not be who I am today and none of this would be possible.

ACKNOWLEDGMENTS & DEDICATIONS

Thank you to my tribe of fierce mamas who inspire me beyond what I ever thought was possible. Thank you for sharing your beautiful souls with the world and for trusting me through this insanely life changing process. I love you all.

Thank you to the mamas out there reading this work. If we can touch the heart of even one person, we have done our job. Please remember that you are amazing!

To Josie Cipriano of Cipriano Palmer Photography for the beautiful headshots and the maternity shoot that made the cover artwork. You have a gift. You are also mama to six little people which actually makes you superhuman! (www.ciprianopalmer.com | https://www.josiecriprianoportraits.com)

Thank you to GBR Publishing House for all of your hard work and dedication to your authors, with a massive shout out to owner and founder Ky-Lee Hanson. Ky-Lee, you really are building something beautiful. Your passion for supporting women to become the best they can be is amazing. Thank you for your leadership, guidance and most of all patience through the learning curves.

Thank you Drew Close for taking on eleventh hour projects and assisting the design team. www.drewclose.com

Thank you to Natalie Dale for your amazing makeup artistry. (www.daley dosefilms.com)

To our very own Lila Beijer for shooting some of the girl's headshots, mamas helping mamas is what the YGT Mama community is all about.

Thank you to Tania and Sheryl for the hard work and sleepless nights your teams put into editing, we sincerely could not have done this without you.

Thank you to Rafael Chimicatti for your brilliant and lightning fast work on the interior typeset design and for picking up any pieces, I have never met you but you are a rockstar. (www.behance.net/chimicatti)

Once again, thank you to my village. My husband for always pushing me to stretch outside of my comfort zone. All the boys amazing aunts, uncles and cousins for loving our children so much. My mom for her raw and soulful contribution to this book and for always being my rock. My dad for the lessons and gifts he likely does not even know he has provided. My grandfather (great-grandpa) for showing me that age is but a number. My boys for teaching me so much every day and helping gain priceless perspective on life. So much love for you all!

Sabrina Greer

Author | Blogger | Mama
Connector of Inspiring Souls | Woman of Many Hats

Sabrina Greer knew from a young age that her life's purpose was to fulfill her three passions: Save the world (philanthropy), see the world (travel), and shape the world (teach and inspire others to be their best selves). Her enthusiasm for life, desire to give back, and stubborn drive to succeed are impenetrable.

Sabrina's journey towards living a life by design and a heart full of love began when she was a young child and her parents decided to become foster parents for predominantly special needs children. She learned compassion, empathy, and a strong devotion for helping others. At the ripe age of fifteen, the next milestone was set in motion when she was offered her first international modeling contract. Not one to ever pass up an adventure, this brave free spirit embarked on what became a ten+ year career as an internationally recognized model, actor, and spokesperson with contracts for major magazines and television productions. During each of her sessions abroad to over twenty countries, she volunteered within the local communities, exercising her passions and doing what she truly loved.

After ten years of globetrotting, Sabrina found home base back in Ontario, Canada (her origin) and decided to earn her degree in education and developmental psychology to accredit her world changing efforts, quickly realizing her superpowers lay in entrepreneurialism and coaching others to discover their potential by sharing opportunity and inspirational writing. Now wife to the man of her dreams and mother to three incredible boys, she spends her days being present, writing books, blogging about life, love and motherhood, all while building a village of people that inspire and set her soul on fire.

www.ygtmama.com
ig: @ygtmama | fb: ygtmama

Golden Brick Road
Publishing House

Locking arms and helping each other down their Golden Brick Road

At Golden Brick Road Publishing House, we lock arms with ambitious people and create success through a collaborative, supportive, and accountable environment. We are a boutique shop that caters to all stages of business around a book. We encourage women empowerment, and gender and cultural equality by publishing single author works from around the world, and creating in-house collaborative author projects for emerging and seasoned authors to join.

Our authors have a safe space to grow and diversify themselves within the genres of poetry, health, sociology, women's studies, business, and personal development. We help those who are natural born leaders, step out and shine! Even if they do not yet fully see it for themselves. We believe in empowering each individual who will then go and inspire an entire community. Our Director, Ky-Lee Hanson, calls this: The Inspiration Trickle Effect.

If you want to be a public figure that is focused on helping people and providing value, but you do not want to embark on the journey alone, then we are the community for you.

To inquire about our collaborative writing opportunities or to bring your own idea into vision, reach out to us at:

www.goldenbrickroad.pub

Goals, Brilliance, and Reinvention

Join us at the social

www.gbrsociety.com

GBR Society is a community of authors, future authors, readers, and supporters. We are connected through Golden Brick Road Publishing House; a leadership, empowerment, and self-awareness publisher. The GBR empire is built on sharing opportunity. It is a brand built on being a true community consisting of friendship, allies, support, advancing with each other, philanthropy, and having each others back. We struggle together and we flourish together. We are a community budding with endless ongoing love. Our authors are real people, continuously looking to grow in their personal and professional lives which also makes them readers and supporters to others in the growing community. We want to make this motivation contagious by inviting you in to meet and grow with us. Get to know the real people behind successful author brands and careers. Build friendships with motivated people and find your own voice. We have been said to be guides in helping others discover their own strength; each person is their own best judge and best healer. No one does it for you, they can only share options with you.

Join us as a reader and gain a wealth of insight from our authors and featured guests, while receiving access to exclusive advanced books, online and in person events, book clubs, summits, online programs, retreats and special offers. Learn from us how to advance in your personal and professional life. Access information on what interests you choosing from health and wellness, sociology, human rights, writing and reading, creating a business, advancing a business or career, and personal development including self-esteem, introspection, self-discovery, and self-awareness.

CPSIA information can be obtained
at www.ICGtesting.com
Printed in the USA
LVOW10s0038080518
576387LV00008B/192/P